MUMMY JOJO
UNCUT

Time for a MOJO injection

JOJO FRASER

Hey,

Welcome to this wonderful book brought to you by That Guy's House Publishing.

At That Guy's House we believe in real and raw wellness books that inspire the reader from a place of authenticity and honesty.

This book has been carefully crafted by both the author and publisher with the intention that it will bring you a glimmer of hope, a rush of inspiration and sensation of inner peace.

It is our hope that you thoroughly enjoy this book and pass it onto friends who may also be in need of a glimpse into their own magnificence.

Have a wonderful day.

Love,

Sean Patrick

That Guy.

I dedicate this book to my Dad, the champagne of the party. Running around Arthur's Seat helped to heal my soul when I missed you. This one's for Arthur the greatest x

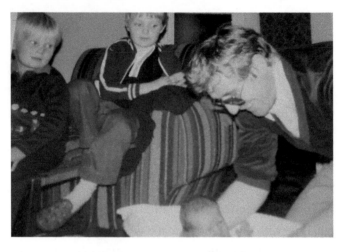

Let me tell you that I love you and
I think about you all the time
Caledonia you're calling me and now I'm going home
But if I should become a stranger you know that it would
make me more than sad
Caledonia's been everything I've ever had

Dougie MacLean

TIME FOR A MOJO INJECTION

12th November 2015

Move over Botox, it's time for a mojo injection. The road to finding it might be painful. It may sting like an actual syringe. I'm talking epidural style. We are going deep.

These critical thoughts I hear are sucking the joy out of my soul. They say happiness looks beautiful. I have to agree. If the secret to happiness is common sense, then why have so many of us lost our mojo? Why are so many of us living smaller than life?

A happy soul glows but my mojo has taken a ride to gloomy town. I want to live a life I love. I want to tell the negative chatterbox in my head to DO ONE. It's a constant daily battle.

Who wins? I decide. Sink or swim?

....

Today

I made a choice that I would swim. I would be the champagne of the party, even when people try to piss all over my picnic. I would judge less, live more and create the greatest story of my life. You coming?

Like an epidural, as terrifying as this process can be – my mojo is back. People tend to notice these things before we do. It shows in our eyes. Wise friends have commented that my eyes light up when I talk. They sparkle. I feel so much lighter. I feel ready to share my journey with you now. It's scary to let it go. I'm nervous, but now is the time to pass over ... the mojo injection.

Meet the Family

Spread love like I'm Paddington Bear

Boston Bun

Fields of Gold Image by Rachael Lynch from Beautiful Bairns Photography.

Great to meet you. I am JoJo Fraser aka 'Mummy JoJo'. I am currently the number one wellness and mental health blogger in Edinburgh and Scotland, according to Google organic search, cheers my old friend. I also held third to fifth for 'perfect Mum' for the majority of 2016/2017. When you read Chapter Three you will get that joke.

Incredible Mojo Image by Rachael Lynch from
Beautiful Bairns Photography.

I adore writing and there has been no stopping me since I was big enough to put pen to paper. My little girl is the same at the tender age of five and it melts my heart. My Mum has countless notepads, filled with 'novels' I wrote as a child. After school many assumed I would go on to drama school. Both writing and being on the stage is where I feel at home and drama worked wonders for my confidence. I was an extremely shy and anxious child.

I chose to complete a Master's in Business and Marketing, but I love how vlogging and content creation has allowed me to become an entertainer again. I love to entertain, and they do say laughter is the medicine of life. I've been a mental health ambassador for the past four years with no intention of stopping. I'm quite frankly blown away by the power of social media. I'm blown away that people struggling with issues such as stress, insecure thoughts, anxiety and extreme depression write to me to tell me I am helping them smile. I love people and I love deep and honest conversation. I have always believed that we need to feel heard. We need to be given a voice. We need to be encouraged to share. This was the reason I launched my podcast – which is also called Mummy JoJo UNCUT, time for a mojo injection. It's a bit like therapy and holds nothing back and I adore it. Tune in anytime. My desire is for this to be a safe place where you laugh and hopefully smile in agreement throughout this read, but a small warning – there is no filter and there may also be some tears.

Meet hubs. He is fun, annoyingly clever, upbeat and has great chat (apart from when he nags).

He has cracking eyes, which he has passed on to the kids. Lucky them. He is addicted to cleaning (I'm glad one of us is), exercise and his family. Hubs gets my passion to smash the stigma of mental health. He too has lived and breathed the devastating impact with his family. He has been my number one support in all the work I am doing. People often ask me if he minds the fact I am so open and honest. He assures me he doesn't.

The focus groups think he comes across well in this book. I think he gets a bit of stick in some of the chapters but the fact he lets me share so much means he is in fact a legend. Even though he annoys the life out of me when he goes on about housework. I'm with JK.

"People very often say to me, 'How did you do it, how did you raise a baby and write a book?' And the answer is – I didn't do housework for four years. I am not superwoman. And, um, living in squalor, that was the answer".

JK Rowling

(Note – this legend is getting two quotes in the book as she once taught me at school, down in Leith and she is a true inspiration).

Meet Bonnie, our five-year-old and little butterfly. She is funny, caring, quirky and better at vlogging than me. In fact, she has won the heart of many across social media and like a butterfly - she can't see her wings. Anxiety runs in the family, but we are working hard to raise her with bags of confidence and kindness. She loves vlogging, taking pictures, writing, reading, dancing and chocolate.

Last but not least meet Charlie who is currently three. He is cheeky, charming, headstrong and very chatty for his age. He loves balls, bats, eating fruit and being in the water, especially a hot bath.

CONTENTS

Sometimes there are no words. Sometimes all we can do is show up and be there. Even if we are not wanted. Never take this personally.

When the shizzle hits the fan we often say, "why is this happening to me?" Bad things happen to everyone. After acceptance we can use the pain to create our own kind of magic.

She may look like super Mum but some just put on a better show. We are all just winging it. Never believe that success is effortless and remember – we all have our own issues. Be kind.

It turns out that looks can be deceiving when it comes to fitness. Strong and healthy is my goal. Always do it for the soul first.

We all have scars, be they physical or mental. Scars tell a story. They make us stronger. Embrace them and NEVER forget the P word.

Enjoy the journey of finding someone special but remember that people will let you down and you will let them down too. Be the champagne of your own party.

Guess who 'the one' really is? It's all a myth.

Handle rejection like a winner
– it's not all about you.

I used to be the queen of excuses. There is a balance between contentment and setting goals that excite us. Be a goal digger.

It can be easy to lose balance with our vices. Life is to be enjoyed with things that give us a buzz, but do we control them, or do they control us?

How do we keep our issues to ourselves when raising kids?

Some real talk about the number one vice that controls so many of us today.

Goal diggers are often busy. Mindfulness can be attainable for the busiest of people.

Do you recognise any of these thoughts? Thoughts that hold you back. Accept them, but they do not define you. You are magic.

"I figure life is a gift and I don't intend on wasting it".

Jack (Titanic)

Hello. Can you feel a song coming on? Which track would you choose? Lionel is a legend but I'm quite partial to Adele, I shall explain why later on.

Thanks so much for being here. Perhaps you have followed me on social media for some time. Maybe we have met before, you may even be a close friend or family member. You may know absolutely nothing about me. That doesn't matter. What matters is that you are here now. High five. I'm going to do my very best to keep you here until the end. I want you here with me because this stuff **really** matters.

This book, my first to publish, is my third baby. I'm calling it baby Arthur. It has taken a heck of a lot of work, hundreds of hours' worth of research, a lot of laughter and a lot of tears. Tears from my own pain and tears I have shed with others who have been brave enough to share with me. I have collaborated with The Mental Health Foundation, Wellness and life coaches, positive psychologists, The Blurt Foundation, Nurses, Doctors and hundreds of people who have seriously lost their mojo and had the courage to speak out to me about it. I have travelled around the globe, been on a three-day mind spa, all about the work of Syd Banks and 'The 3 Principles'. I have explored the way our thoughts work. I have practiced a lot of the theory. I have been hypnotised several times. I have explored intense transformational coaching. It's been a mind-blowing journey.

I am not here to ram statistics down your throat, we all know those are terrifying and heart-breaking and I want to make you feel better not worse. Nor am I here to talk through various academic papers and studies that I have researched. I am aware that many of us crave an easy read. Something we can get lost in. I am here to keep it very real. Some call it 'mental health reality TV'. I invite you to have a laugh on me and my issues, because laughing is a fabulous form of therapy.

I ditched the sofa for a marathon medal during this journey and in many ways, writing this book has been a personal marathon.

I passionately believe it is possible to be living in our full mojo, even when life gets a bit too heavy. I have witnessed it first hand, personally and through all those I have worked with and am working with now.

It is possible to get our mojo back even when we are mentally, emotionally, spiritually or physically fragile. There is no magic switch though and often it is a journey. It also takes a conscious effort to replace our negative thoughts with positive ones. It takes a support network too. I want to be part of your support network. I really care. It's part of who I am and my core values, and I hope I can nurture my own mental health so that this passion never leaves me. I invite you to come for the ride with me and let me inject a bit of mojo back if it is prone to going for a walk or a marathon.

I have written this book with a deep-rooted passion in my soul. I have a vision that keeps me awake at night. A vision that one day soon it will be normal to talk openly about mental health and our struggles. A vision that we will learn to start judging less and living more. This starts with being kinder to ourselves. Us humans on planet earth are a lot more similar than we think. I hope you relate to the words. Although your story will be different to mine, I hope you can take some comfort and have a laugh with me. Because when we take ourselves too seriously, that is often when it all goes a bit tits up.

When I was at school not so long ago, cough cough nineteen years, some kids made fun of me for 'smiling too much'. I have always been pigeon-holed as 'the happy one'. Looking back, I was a little embarrassed about it but now I am that bit older and wiser I realise that this was the biggest compliment anyone could give me.

Our Head Teacher gave me a note on my last day at school when I was seventeen. It said:

"You have a sincere and glowing smile that could light up the world and a lovely personality, you will go far".

I vowed the day I got that letter that I would no longer be ashamed for trying to be positive as often as possible. I would ignore the comments about being a 'geek' and a 'teacher's pet'. What was so wrong with being happy anyway?

The truth is, despite being dubbed as 'the happy, positive one', I still have issues. We all do. For a start, I have battled with anxiety for most of my life. Don't get me started on my desire to be a people pleaser to the point I took kindness too far and became a doormat.

Until 2014, I took my mental health for granted. I simply got out of bed each day, being what many call 'larger than life', with the odd blip, anxiety attack and panic over things that didn't really matter. (Note: larger than life is a silly expression – life is large and amazing. Especially when we are living in our mojo).

Why in the UK do we often shy away from being overtly positive? Why was I heckled for being happy? I did a poll across social media and roughly 70% said that happy people are infectious, they glow, they feel good to be around. The others responded with:

- — All this wellness hype is a little self-indulgent.

- — Super positive people are too intense for me.

- — Happy people can come across as fake and patronising.

- — There is no such thing as a free lunch JoJo! Don't trust anyone.

- — Some people get a better head start in life.

WOW! Winge, winge, groan, groan. We all have these critical thoughts within us. We doubt others, we doubt ourselves.

People dub me as 'the positive blogger', the 'bubbly one'. You want to know why? I said SHUT IT to the inner critic in me and the voice that is prone to judgement of others. I said piss off to perceptions. My mojo is back, it's like a huge weight has shifted from my shoulders. I feel lighter.

I can tell when someone has got their mojo because I can see it in their eyes. Just like Sandy, my Head Teacher could see in mine.

The difference between now and nineteen years ago is that I am no longer ashamed.

Nineteen years ago, I WAS ASHAMED OF BEING HAPPY??!! What was I thinking?!

The state of being happy is a very personal thing, we all have different things that excite us. We are all just winging this thing called life and we are all mentally fragile. Our anxiety and stress levels can fluctuate like the stock market. Even the happiest of people need a toolkit. I see self-development as part of my daily 'to-do' list. It is very easy to slip back into old habits but living in our full mojo feels so much better.

Things are changing slowly but surely. This decade is all about focusing on our minds as much as our bodies. What was once taboo is becoming cool. This needed to happen. Keep calm and carry on doesn't work for everyone, especially when it comes to our mental health.

Mental wellness is no longer reserved for those in straitjackets, foaming at the mouth. If you have watched my vlogs across social media you probably think I am mental. Damn right I am, we are all mental because we all have a mind. Mental wellness impacts each and every one of us. So much so that the royal family are talking about it now. This excites me. It's time to normalise discussions about our minds. It's time to make the self-help section bigger and cooler. It's time for more voices, more love, more passion for 'living as large as life can be'. It's time to make mental wellness interesting, real and relatable. Less facts and figures, more real-life examples. It's time to stop making positive people feel weird and 'too large' for life. There is no such thing.

When life started to feel really sad, I decided to use the emotional pain I was feeling to help others. I started my wellness blog, which Bonnie (who was two at the time) named 'Mummy JoJo'. I had no idea what that journey would involve, but without worrying too much I just pulled a 'Nike' and bashed on.

I remember the first raw and brutally honest piece of writing I published online about mental health. I had tears flooding down my face as I typed it, praying that it would help even one person. That piece was read by over twenty-six thousand people. It opened up the wonderful opportunity to meet and collaborate with those who have experienced trauma; grief of the worst kind, abuse, mental illnesses and broken hearts.

I get to work with incredible people who have found their purpose and are now glowing with their own mojo. They are scarred and vulnerable but their eyes sparkle. They are desperate to help others and make a change which I find so beautiful. They are as large as life. Plus, if you have seen the mental health stats you will be more than aware that we need as many people like this as possible.

I was once a very naïve person who thought you could tell people struggling with their mental health to 'pull themselves together'. Judge JoJo was not living in her full mojo. Then my best friend, my Dad, got sick. He was diagnosed with severe depression.

Life was hard. The glowing happy soul, my sweet Pop, was suffering. We almost lost him to a horrible illness. Thankfully we came out the other side of it as a family. We learnt so much.

Whilst there is no tangible mojo injection available, there are so many toolkits to help us feel happy within ourselves and start to glow. That starts with the decision to try.

I have used a lot of those toolkits to overcome my battle with anxiety. I have been living and breathing all things wellness, mindfulness and happiness the past four years. Because my happiness and smile are no longer things I take for granted. I have seen a smile that could light up the world fade into darkness.

What I say, or even better sing is:

"If you're happy and you know it clap your freaking hands and wave them high"

Now twerk, squat, shake and dance. You are happy? You have found your mojo? I salute you because what an incredible way to live this incredibly fast but often magical journey.

If you have not yet found that mojo and are prone to listening to the inner critic in you then it's time to get comfortable. If you are prone to judging others then go grab a drink, light a candle and jump in the bath. Whatever floats that sweet boat of yours and let's get started. I want to meet you, say, "hello mojo" and see those eyes sparkle because it feels SO good. Note: booze and caffeine are best enjoyed in moderation, but like anything in life we all need a bit of balance.

CHAPTER 1

WHEN THE MOJO GOES OUT OF TOWN – THIS ONE'S FOR ARTHUR

"It's so difficult to explain depression to someone who's never been there, because it's not just sadness".

JK Rowling

March 2015

Dad,

I know you don't want to talk to me right now. I worry you are upset with me. Should I have visited you in hospital more? Are you annoyed we let them take you there? We hated having to do it, but you were not safe at home.

I worry about you. It's so scary. I hate it. You don't belong there. I want to see you back at home with Mum. I miss you so much.

I miss our chats. I miss your hugs. I miss all the laughs we used to have. I want you to know that no matter what you have said I will never stop loving you, Dad. I am your little girl and I always will be. You may have changed but I will always be there if you need me. I just want to see you smile again.

Please don't be ashamed. I know you are, but you should never be. It's not your fault. There are a lot of people that still don't understand that a mental illness requires just as much compassion as a physical one.

You are still my hilarious, clever, caring, thoughtful, wonderful Dad. You are just fragile right now. I can see it in your eyes and I feel so powerless.

Dad, I won't give up on you because I know you would never give up on me. When I see you get better, and I pray you will get better, Dad, I promise that I shall cherish every smile, every laugh and every hug. Somehow through this awful time I am going to have to learn to swim. Even if I want to sink because life is so sad without the real you right now. I just want to be your perfect little girl again. I wish you would let me. Depression isn't sadness and anxiety is as real as the pain in my heart. I get it now. Dad, I am so like you in so many ways. I get how lost, alone and very afraid you must feel.

JoJo xx

I am a third child. My parents had two boys first and my Mum was happy to quit at that. As a Mum of two I get that. Life is magical yet mental with two young kids. My Dad wanted a little girl though. He talked my Mum round and there I was. His wish was granted – whoop, thanks for having me folks, I am sure it was hard work but quite frankly I am delighted to be here. (Small print – of course, if I was a little Joe instead I'm sure he would have been just as happy because we fall in love with people and character, not gender).

My Dad got his little girl he could push on the swings. They called me Joanne but when I was a little baby he held me in his arms, looked at me and said 'you're a JoJo'. My Dad tragically lost his eyesight when he was nineteen and my Mum, who he was dating at the time, was his rock. Despite not being able to see me clearly that morning he held me, he could sense that I was a JoJo. From that moment on I was his JoJo. A lot of my friends and family won't know this, but whenever anyone calls me 'Joanne' it makes me feel uncomfortable. I'm with Dad – I'm a JoJo. Ironically, Hubs continues to call me Joanne out of habit, he loves the name. As a result, people that tune into my 'Insta stories' have started a # - #don'tcallmejoanne. I digress.

Dad worshipped me. I was the apple of his eye. The bond between a father and his little girl is really quite magical. I watch hubs with Bonnie and it really is something else.

Dad also calls me WYSIWYG (pronounced whizzywig). It means 'What You See is What You Get'.

The thing is, things have changed now. My Dad, my best friend, currently wants nothing to do with me and it is breaking my heart.

I am sitting in the Royal Edinburgh hospital and I feel scared and confused. How has it come to this? I am holding Charlie who is around eight weeks old. I can hardly recognise the man in front of me. He's now six stone instead of his usual twelve. He doesn't have the strength to talk. He seems annoyed we are even here. I have just driven to the hospital, with my hungry milk monster baby screaming for my crazy milk filled boobs in the back of the car for half an hour. All for what? To be told to "go away" by the person who thought the absolute world of me just two months ago. This man who was once my loving, funny and caring Dad is ignoring me. He is ignoring his grandchild and his Son in Law that he recently said was "meant for me". This should be the happiest time of my life. My Dad should be celebrating with us over the birth of our new baby. The problem is he can't be happy about anything. Not even the beautiful little grandson called Charlie he has always wanted. Charlie was always his favourite name, but my Mum didn't want it for their two boys, my big brothers. She was never a big fan of Prince Charles.

Sadly, one in four of us will experience some form of mental illness. Sometimes grief or trauma will trigger it, other times it can come from being overworked or it may be years of neglect. Stress is often the starter

4

before the depressive monster jumps in as a huge main course, dessert and perhaps even a huge plate of cheese, chilli jam and artisan breads. Often it can appear out of nowhere and mental illnesses can attack the people we least expect. My wonderful, sweet Pop was one of those people.

When he felt the signs coming on he was too embarrassed to talk. That is the normal reaction, sadly, especially for men. We don't like to let people down, we try to stay strong. We don't share our problems in the UK. Initially he felt off. A bit like I feel when I am going through PMS. I question myself, my parenting and sometimes my life. I have days that I feel out of my depth. I am impatient and grumpy. I lose my balance. I feel sad even when I have so much to be happy about. Then hubs will say, "what is wrong with you?", whilst no doubt feeling tempted to download Tinder, and I realise it is *that* time of the month. Hormones do funny things to us. Do you know the GP's offer antidepressants for PMS now? I'm scared of them, though.

There is still an attitude of 'pull yourself together' and get on with it. This can be destructive. If you are having a day where you feel emotionally flat, a day where crying is all too easy then the last words you want to hear are 'chin up'. Wow, thanks for those wise words - I am OK now and totally loving life. High-freaking-five to the judgemental critics in us. The critics who tell someone having a full-blown anxiety attack to 'stay calm'. Yeah right. I was once one of those judgemental people and this kind of behaviour pulled me so far away from my mojo. Judge JoJo was not living in her full mojo.

Mental health makes many of us feel awkward. For some time, my Dad put on a front when he was with people, he was in 'overcompensation' mode. He felt too ashamed to admit how he was really feeling. This is the normal response.

My Dad is hilarious. He reminds me of the late legend Robin Williams, funnily enough he looks a bit like him too. He has battled with anxiety for most of his life. I have picked that up too, but anxiety is so much more common than we let on.

Mental health impacts us all, because we all have a mind. A mind that is as precious as our bodies. It is easy to laugh off these pressures in public. They do say that laughter is the medicine of life. We are often encouraged to surround ourselves with positive people who lift us up. But sometimes we need to accept that we need help. We need to accept that laughter isn't always enough. We need to accept that sometimes we cannot be glowing with the mojo. We also need to remember that the most positive people are just as vulnerable.

My Dad got scared and he tried to talk. He was trying to rationalise his irrational thoughts. Of course, the judges came out and said, "pull yourself together; you have a beautiful family and a great life". He couldn't though. Sometimes people are too sick to just pull themselves together, or far too sad. Sometimes this thing called life gets too heavy, nobody is invincible. Depression and mental health do not discriminate. They don't care how you look, what you earn, how beautiful your kids are, how amazing your partner is (my Mum is an angel sent from above) or how amazing your life appears to be.

So now here I am, sat in a scary hospital staring at a stranger. The medication they are giving him is making him so much worse. Which is why I fear it and would prefer to try and manage my PMS in other ways.

The doctors have absolutely no clue what to do. My family feel so helpless. My best friend; the life and soul of the party, my caring, funny, intelligent, interesting, interested Dad is gone. We are left with his body and another person. His mind is broken and the doctors can't fix him. I didn't know it was possible to experience grief while a person was here on this earth. I am so very sad. He thinks he is in a prison. He needs to be here though. He is not safe at home right now.

I feel so angry that my kids are being robbed of such a fun, hands-on granddad that has so much to teach them and so much to make them laugh about. I feel pain in my chest and a hard lump forming in my throat. I really am fighting with all my might to hold back the tears. I feel helpless. I can't get through to him. Should I get a letter written up in braille and leave it with him? A letter telling him how loved he is? The thing is, he doesn't want help. He has given up. Would he just throw it in the bin?

After ten minutes of him asking us to 'just go' I give my Dad a big hug and we leave.

As we get in the car feeling deflated hubs says:

"I understand darling. I have been here. It was the same with my Mum when I was a boy and when I was a teenager. You need to believe that he can get better. No matter how hard he tries to push us away - we will keep going. My Mum got better, so can your Dad".

He gets it. He is my rock when I am starting to lose faith. He is the mojo injection that I need that day.

The months go by and we keep going. I have started running and sometimes I run 8k home from the hospital to clear my head and take some calm time to deal with what is happening. Sometimes I take the kids in to try and make him laugh. The hospital is full of people on a high and they often passionately throw money at me for the kids and tell me to get them something nice. You see, young children are magical. They are wonderful and simply magical.

Dad starts to feel strong enough to go for a slow walk in the hospital grounds, which are full of bunnies hopping around. I start to find a way to communicate with him again. He has remembered his love for chocolate. He is learning to enjoy something again. It's a small step and it's fantastic to see him eating. I want him to gain weight so I can recognise him again.

He has not called me JoJo in over a year and it hurts. I long to hear him say the simple words he always says with so much love: "Hello JoJo".

9ᵗʰ April 2017

One For Arthur Becomes a Grand National Treasure for Scotland

My Dad got out of hospital. He started smiling again and slowly gained a healthy weight. They finally found some medication that helped.

This whole experience has taught me so much. It has taught me that it takes courage to talk openly. It takes strength to open up and say, "I need help". What terrifies me the most is that so many people feel so helpless by trying to keep calm and carry on that they give up. How have we let it get to this?

I am ready to enter a new age of wellness and self-care. An age where we say, "deep breaths and talk about it". We need to feel supported. We need to know that crying is OK. We need to stop judging. We need to take time to understand how vulnerable yet magical our minds are.

There have been so many times I have tried my hardest to hold back tears in front of people. Reading a good book, listening to a beautiful talk or getting lost in a movie. I just wanted to totally get lost in it, release all that tension in my throat and cry it out. I felt stupid though. It would make people feel really weird. Ouch. Holding in tears actually really hurts.

Today on the 9ᵗʰ of April, I cried a lot of tears. They were happy tears and I had goose pimples down my spine. I was home with Dad and my family. We were getting ready to watch The Grand National, which is the only time in the year I like to place a bet. The year previous, I had betted on my marathon date number which also happens to be Dad's birthday. Number 29. That horse won when nobody saw it coming. The money was nice but it was symbolic to me and meant so much more than money. Some things money can't buy.

On this day, 9th April 2017 there was a horse called 'One For Arthur', so despite the low odds it was a no brainer that this horse would be my bet.

Of course, he wasn't going to win though. The odds were so low. One for Arthur struggled to go the strong pace for the first mile. In fact, nobody saw him on the screen or heard his name the entire race. Dad was looking a little deflated. You see, he always thinks of others. He felt bad I would lose my money simply because I wanted to bet on his name. I didn't care about the money though. I cared about my Dad. I was happy he had pulled through and something inside me told me that so would One For Arthur. It would be a sign from the universe or God, whatever you believe, that we had won a great race. The race of learning to embrace our mental health. We found hope, because believe me, if you had seen my Dad in hospital at his worst, my family needed a whole lot of hope.

When absolutely nobody saw it coming, One For Arthur finished in first place, he ran as fast as a bullet. At one stage he was twenty lengths back behind the pace-setting Rogue Angel, but he steadily crept into the contest helped by some superb jumping. I screamed and grabbed my Dad. It was a symbolic moment which made it beautiful and as I held him I let the tears stream down my face.

In March 2015 as I held my Dad's hand in hospital, he told me he wasn't going to live to see his sixty-fifth birthday at the end of the month. He looked so broken and so fragile that I believed him. He pulled through though. It was a miracle. Just like One For Arthur. My Dad was beaming and he shouted out loud, **"yes JoJo!"**

This letter has been adapted from a very popular blog I wrote that was shared by The Blurt Foundation in 2016. It was a letter that I wrote on behalf of my Dad. A letter that I knew he would have written for me, had he been made aware of what was about to happen. A letter that I want my kids to read if this ever happens to me, because I am so very like my Dad.

Please Stay and Hold my Hand

My little JoJo,

I love you so much. Never ever forget this. You will always be my little girl. You have children of your own now, so I know you finally understand the depth of my love for you.

It pains me to my core to write this but soon things will change. I am not going to be able to show you how much I love you. I am going to push you away. I am going to tell you to stay away from me. I am going to say scary things I don't mean. I am going to get so paranoid about so many things. I am going to stop enjoying life. I wish this wasn't so. I wish I could stop it. All I want to do is see you smile, laugh and have fun. I want to enjoy my beautiful family and grandchildren. If I tell you to go away please try not to get upset. I am so ashamed I just don't want you seeing me so unwell. I am trying to protect you the way I know best.

There will be nothing you can say to make me feel better. Believe me, the Doctors will try to fix me. Just sit and hold my hand. I will tell you I don't, but I need you JoJo. I also need time. Try and have a little patience. This will be so very hard for you, I know that because you are just like me. Fill your time with something that heals your soul. Run, write, help others and light those up with that beautiful smile. I am sorry I am not going to be able to appreciate it.

None of this is your fault precious. Please never blame yourself. Please be strong for the family. It is going to be so hard for everyone. I love you all so much and it breaks my heart that you will have to see me this way. Don't give up hope, even if I do. Keep believing in me, please. I need you to believe in me. I need you to believe I can get better. I need you to never forget who I really am. Always keep the real me close to your heart. You will ALWAYS be my perfect little girl.

Most importantly, stop being so hard on yourself.

I will love you forever my little WYSIWYG. Pop x

Thanks so much to all my amazing readers for all the fantastic feedback you have given me on my writing, speaking and video content.

Here are a few extracts from some amazing people who have written to me.

"Depression can hit anyone at any time, and when I was at my lowest after having my son I told the Dr that if it wasn't for my son then I wouldn't get out of bed, he said well thank God for your son. And I do every single day I thank God for my son. He has been my greatest teacher in so many unexpected ways.

There is so much stigma attached around mental health and that's why I am inspired by you JoJo for being open and sharing your experiences and encouraging everyone to find wellbeing for themselves".

"Mummy JoJo: I suffered from severe PND (slowly recovering) and I am in awe of the work you do. I think that sharing our journey is so important. I felt so isolated during the worst of my days. Reading about others who had survived and come to enjoy life again offered me a small consolation. These excerpts are very real for me. You are doing a wonderful thing here. Thank you".

"WOW. Having suffered with mental health myself I have read a lot about depression. This is by far the most powerful piece I have ever read. Thank you".

"This has definitely made me feel more sympathetic towards those who are struggling. Thank you for helping me to see depression from a new perspective".

"My experience with depression was to be stuck in a place where instead of enjoying who I was and what I had I was regretting everything that did not turn out the way I wanted yet. A bit later in my journey I found that actually my whole emotional base that I thought was solid was just a pile of broken heart pieces".

"Medication helped me the first time I went into depression, but I think at the same time it prevented me from facing the pile of heart splinters. The second time it's the love and compassion shared with my best friend that made the difference and this time I'm able to face my wounds and pains with her help".

"Exploring the broken pieces is what really brings lasting relief and allows healing and rediscovering that we are perfect already if we peel away the layers of illusions about what we should be".

"When my depression gets very bad my whole being becomes drawn in, physically as well as mentally and emotionally. I hardly speak and don't want to be in company, isolating myself, yet also I am desperate for human interaction and help. It is so comforting to have someone to put an arm round my shoulder or just squeeze my hand. No words needed at all...but at the same time tells me so much and I feel love".

"Know that feeling and needing to be hugged but not wanting people near me. We must erase the stigma of mental illness, we need to talk about it. Just knowing

others go through the same when u don't understand what's happening to you is so helpful".

"It really touched me immeasurably to read this"

"These are all completely justified feelings - it's strange how depression can rocket us into unexpected emotional places or leave us feeling completely numb".

"Mummy JoJo, this blog is probably the most accurate thing I've read on Social Media. Hand holding helps you and them so perfectly".

TOOLKIT

If someone you love is struggling with their mental health, there is often nothing you can do but just show up. They will not want to burden you with it. They will often push you away. It is so hard. Let those you care for know that you're there for them.

If you are caring for someone you love who is suffering from a mental illness such as depression or anxiety, you most certainly need support. It's an extremely hard time. To quote my beautiful Mum:

"I wouldn't wish this on my worst enemy".

There is no sugar coating it. Depression is real, it's dark. Too many beautiful souls are taken by it, my Dad was very nearly one of them and writing these words breaks my heart.

As a carer it is terrifying leaving someone alone when they have such dark thoughts. Ask for help from family, friends or carers so you can do simple things like going to get your hair cut or doing a weekly food shop.

It can be so easy to take things personally. Remember that a mental illness is the same as a physical one. It requires as much compassion. Telling someone to 'pull themselves together' won't work or help. The person living with the mental health condition needs to want to get help. You can't force them.

There are so many cases of anxiety and depression that have not been diagnosed. This is hugely down to the stigma that is sadly still associated with mental health. Perhaps someone you love is pushing you away right now and you are blaming yourself, like many of us do. It can be easy to take these symptoms personally.

Some of the warning signs of depression are feeling:

- Extremely upset and irritable
- Distracted and unable to concentrate
- Slow and sluggish or agitated and excitable
- Disinterested in things once enjoyed
- Changes in appetite, with weight gain or loss
- Liable to cry at any given moment
- Restless and unable to sleep
- Worthless, unhelpful or unattractive
- Frustrated when even small things go wrong
- Unable to muster the energy to get through the day
- Cut off from friends and family
- Isolated and alone

If you think you may be suffering from depression or another mental health condition then please share. Book an appointment with your GP, talk to someone. Sharing is a sign of strength, never a weakness. Even if you can share with just one person you trust, it could make a huge difference.

We are all prone to dark thoughts. They can be terrifying, but remind yourself that they are just a thought. We all experience thoughts, but they do not have to define us. We don't have to act on our thoughts.

Try and find hope. People can get better. It takes a whole lot of patience, perseverance and commitment to care for someone who is mentally broken. I heard a statistic recently that said 70% of people recover from depression.

Don't forget who you are. Try and channel the pain into something creative. Writing and running were hobbies that got me through the dark days.

Sometimes you will get a sign from the universe and 9th April 2017 was one of those moments for me. When it happens just stop and embrace the magic. Don't be ashamed to cry tears of happiness or sadness.

"You will never understand a mental health illness if you've never suffered it, and it's OK not to understand it. Listen. Be available and just listen to what your loved one is saying. Encourage appropriate help, but you cannot force it. Encourage them to find something to engage with, a sport, hobby, something to focus their mind on during difficult times.

When they seem withdrawn, let them know you are there. Let them know you care about them and that they are loved and not alone. Popping round for a coffee or sending a card or text is sometimes more than enough. Don't judge. Supporting someone with mental health problems can be frustrating, but you have to remember that it's the illness that is making them act the way they are. With the appropriate help, things can get better. It's all about balance. It very easy to just want to 'fix someone' but you must remember to take care of yourself too. You cannot be there for someone if you aren't looking after your own mental health. Remember, you cannot cure someone with a mental health problem. They have to want to get better and be ready to accept help. That is when you can be there to support and help".

Suzy Campbell (Forever_a_mum)

CHAPTER 2

FLY HIGH BUTTERFLY - ACCEPTANCE ADELE STYLE

"There's no greater power,
than the power of goodbye".
Madonna

August 2017

Dear Mummy,

I love you so much. I never ever want you to die. But if you have to then please can we die together?

Bonnie (age five)

As we have touched on, bad things can happen. I will never forget crying so hard I struggled to breathe when I watched a video of my Dad telling me how proud he was of me on my wedding day. To quote:

"This girl you have here is my world. She is my little JoJo. She constantly thinks of other people and her smile lights me up".

Who would have thought that as little as three years later he would become a stranger? He would push me away. It happened though, and I had to deal with it. Yes, the tears were flowing hard. Sometimes it was hard to stop. Sadness is a natural energy and I find it beautiful. How amazing to love a person that much they can bring you to floods of tears? I also cherish every hug and hold him that bit tighter now that he is in a much better place. I cherish every beautiful word that comes out of his mouth. The guy has top banter.

I decided to channel all of my hurt and negative energy into something creative. I have never looked back and I am thankful every single day for the people I have met since launching Mummy JoJo back in November 2015.

It is possible to do amazing things when we feel sad or angry. Being overwhelmed with sadness is a normal part of life. Death is sadly also a normal part of life. It is something that we have to accept. As is saying goodbye. I'm with Madonna: there is no greater power than the power of goodbye.

When life gets heavy it can hit us a bit like a tidal wave. Songs sound different. Food tastes different. People can make us mad, especially the happy ones, with the glowing mojo eyes. I get that. Sometimes it is impossible for our eyes to sparkle.

Life can get heavy. People break our hearts, we lose people we love. Stress can become chronic and relationships change. Depression is a nasty monster. To be frank - shit happens and sometimes it feels way too heavy to be reminded that 'time's a healer'.

The truth is, time of course is a healer (and sometimes that involves medication and/or therapy too). It depends how heavy the load is but feeling anger, fear and sadness is never something we should be ashamed of. Nor is feeling overwhelmed and fragile.

Let me ask - how full is your cup right now? Go on, give that cup a mark out of ten and be honest.

I remember one morning my cup was a big fat zero. Dad was really sick. Mum was frazzled. Bonnie was two, Charlie was a few days old and I had what is actually a medical term 'the baby blues'. I was feeling happy and high in many ways but with an extreme dose of 'milk coming in' hormones and lack of sleep, and I was as fragile as a raver after a four-day bender at Glastonbury.

I felt guilty I wasn't giving Bonnie as much attention as normal, we were adapting to life with two small kids. Charlie was feeding all day. Bonnie had picked up on this, how clever are kids? She was milking it (just like her baby brother) and would say:

"Mummy, don't you love me anymore? I miss you".

I missed my Mum and Dad. I felt guilty I couldn't help Mum care for Dad. I felt mad that life had robbed me of a set of incredible grandparents at the most magical time. A time I needed them. Hubs had woken on the wrong side of bed and was being a bit of a knob.

We all have our own issues and battles to ride with. That morning one of my best friends arrived to see me and she was having a tough morning. She needed me. She was feeling anxious. Anxiety is a lot more common than we let on. She felt able to confide in me about her feelings. This would normally have been fine. I love it when people share. I am a great listener. I love to help people. But my cup was running on empty and I had **nothing left to give**. I broke down in floods of tears and my poor friend got the shock of her life. Not Mrs Mojo?! What? That doesn't happen to people like me. I give out mojo injections. In a way it helped my friend to take her mind off the anxiety. Distraction and helping others is always great for our mental health.

You are not invincible, please don't forget to top up that cup with self-care. Self-care to me is like washing. We need a little bit of it daily and sometimes we need to go for the full-on bubble bath before we reach breaking point.

Perhaps overnight it has gone from nicely full to hollow and smashed into thousands of tiny pieces. Be it gradual or a sudden slap hard in the face, we need to be diagnosed with time. Time to sleep. Time in hospital getting care. Time to go for a run if we are able. Time alone with a baby and no toddlers, husbands, in laws, friends. Time to cry. Time to punch a boxing bag instead of a person. Time to accept things.

Acceptance is a really beautiful thing when it happens. This occurs when we choose not to box feelings. We need to accept that grief is a normal part of life and it hurts in places we didn't know could exist. It can be crushing. We need to accept that we just had some scary news and we are overwhelmed with the fear of 'what if'. We need to accept that the person we loved was screwing someone else, that person we trusted let us down. We need to accept that childhood wasn't always easy. We need to accept that depression is real and terrifying. We need to accept that we were abused and we blamed ourselves for too long. We were too young to understand and we let fear stop us from getting help. We need to accept that we had a miscarriage or a stillbirth as we watch our friends embrace their baby. We need to accept that we are struggling to conceive and we may never be able to naturally. We need to accept that we lost that job and things are a bit stretched. We need to accept that there was that awful car, plane, train, road accident. We need to accept that our ex-boyfriend is now being really nasty and threatening to upload dodgy videos to social media. We need to accept that we are prone to addictive behaviour. We need to accept how we look and what skills and gifts and weaknesses we were born with. We need to accept who we are. Whatever that journey is – we need to accept the things that we cannot control. **Accept all of it. What matters is now. Right now, in this moment.**

We all have times of pain and suffering but there comes a point when we need to live again, because we don't know our own life sentence. This life has the potential to be so very wonderful and so very beautiful. This life has the potential to be filled with wonderful moments. Moments that are worthy of tears rolling down our face. One for Arthur kind of moments.

Once you have taken time to heal - do you accept what has happened? Are you thankful to have loved? Are you thankful for memories? Memories of a richer life experience from those who played an incredible part? Are you thankful that whatever happened has taught you something? Maybe you are thankful for an amazing therapist or coach, a caring friend or simply thankful that you are still alive. Being thankful helps us get the mojo back. It brightens up our eyes.

I wrote a poem for Bonnie when she started school. It was called 'Fly High my Little Butterfly'. Bonnie is not a fan of wasps, they are so annoying. They buzz, buzz around and leave their germs over our food. They are the middle finger up to our family picnic. Recently, Bonnie and I were belting out 'A Million Dreams' from the Greatest Showman. We were singing it like it was our last morning on the planet. Hubs came out of the shower and pulled the windows open. The sun was beaming in. Bonnie was being a beautiful butterfly – she couldn't see her wings but the truth be told I had tears in my eyes as she belted out:

'Cause every night I lie in bed
The brightest colours fill my head
A million dreams are keeping me awake
I think of what the world could be
A vision of the one I see
A million dreams is all it's gonna take
A million dreams for the world we're gonna make'

What powerful words. This song is 100% a mojo injection in our house. Suddenly – not one, not two, BUT three wasps flew into the room and buzzed all over our perfect sing song. If only it had been butterflies. Butterflies make us feel good. They add colour to our picnic and sing song. They rise above us and spread their beautiful magic.

Can you think of friends, family members and colleagues that spend the majority of their time buzzing at you like a wasp? We are all capable of being a wasp or a butterfly. A wasp finds acceptance so hard. They allow the anger to control them for longer than it should.

When we get criticism, we can get so defensive. If something goes wrong we look for someone to blame. We feel like the world is against us.

Then there are the butterflies that fly high and rise above it. They say yes to life. When life gets a bit too heavy, they think 'cool, how can I learn from this'. If someone complains about something they apologise and ask what they can do to help. Team butterfly want to know how they can make something positive out of an awful situation. When they experience grief, which is sadly part of life, they cry. They feel enormous pain and take time to grieve but they channel that energy into something incredible. They are full of a wonderful feeling of gratitude, to have felt so much love. Butterflies fly high and they are so beautiful.

Adele is a butterfly who accepted. She accepted that she had her heart smashed into thousands of pieces. Then she woke up from the pain and started living. She used her pain to create the most incredible music. Music that helped and is still helping to heal the broken hearts of the world. Music that unites us and reminds us to wish nothing but the best for those we loved. Those who didn't want us. Because never mind, we shall find someone like them. Butterflies inject colour and make us go wow. They have the mojo glow.

I decided I wanted to start flying high, despite the wasps that would get in my way. I wanted to accept life – all of it. The good, the bad, the ugly. I work with people who have accepted it and I get to see their faces light up when they can use their pain to heal and help others. They choose love over anger and that is the most beautiful thing to see. We all have a choice. I know which way I would rather go. I much prefer to focus on the beautiful butterflies over the wasps buzzing all over our family picnic.

Acceptance is a very special part of that kit to get you back, living large like life with that glowing mojo. Accepting that sometimes bad things happen. Accepting that life can be a bitch. Accepting that there are some things we can change and some we can't. Acceptance of yourself, that this is where you are just now but it's not where you're going to be forever, so it's OK to accept it for the moment.

So often when life gets a bit too heavy we put on a front. We act like everything is fine. We fight these feelings and hide our pain even when **it really is OK not to be OK.**

When we experience grief or trauma, we need to accept it. We need to cry and feel the pain. That pain may never go but it will feel lighter. You will learn to smile and laugh again.

As for the daily stresses of life, those little things that build. People can promise us the world and let us down. People can say nasty things. Things out of our control may not always go to plan. Accept it.

No one experience we have on this earth is the be all and end all to life, otherwise you wouldn't be here reading this. So even if you are struggling with acceptance right now, even if someone or something has really got under your skin: you can find a way back.

Sometimes we need reminded that it is possible to do amazing things when we feel sad or angry. It can be hard to truly accept things, and not over-analyse or keep asking why or thinking of things you could have done differently. Give yourself a bit of a break. Ignore the voices that whisper, "I wish I didn't feel like this" and listen to this:

This is how I feel, it doesn't make me a bad person.

Accept these thoughts, let them in, feel them and then see if you can move past them.

Accept other people. If someone shows you who they are, accept it. Accept people as they are, and don't expect anything different. Accept the good and the bad. Accept it. All of it. Don't waste your energy trying to change someone or trying to please them. People will only change if they really want to.

Some parents tell me they struggle to accept their babies growing up. I get that. Saying yes to goodbye can be hard. Parenting is hard but it is magical. When Bonnie started school, part of me was overcome with emotion. My baby was ready to enter a new era. She was excited, she didn't need me. She skipped into school, said hello to her new teacher and didn't even look back. I felt a pang of pain inside. I felt a lump in my throat. I could have let those thoughts breed but I just accepted them. I let them in.

Hubs drove me to George Street and I ordered a cappuccino and a pain au chocolat from a beautiful coffee shop called Burr & Co (it looks a bit like a designer handbag store from the front). Good coffee always makes me smile. I was feeling emotional but I told myself that it was time to let Bonnie go. It was time to allow her space to learn and grow. It was time to trust her. Trust that she would eat her lunch, wash her hands after she had been to the toilet. Trust that she would be kind to people. Trust that she would tell me if anyone hurt her.

Life happens, and acceptance is a daily battle. I say, accept like Adele and go on and do something magical. Something as large as this very beautiful life. Use your talents and do it. Do what you are amazing at as often as you can and create your own kind of magic. Fly high like a butterfly.

Dear Bonnie,

My darling girl. I hope I stay here for so much longer. There is still so much I want to do.

I am feeling emotional today. You started school and I had to ask myself: am I ready to let you go? OK, maybe I'm overreacting. It's not like you are moving out. School though, really? That seemed so far away.

Daddy and I met with your lovely key-worker last week. We discussed how you love to write. The first day I watched you write your name it really hit me how much you have grown up. My baby can write real words.

You can count very high too. We discussed your amazing memory, that will definitely help you with all those exams. You most certainly get that from me but after kids that may go. Don't worry, it is perfectly normal and it is called baby brain.

Whilst I am so proud of all those things you have learned and will continue to learn, there was something that really got to me. Something that matters the most above everything. The section of the report about your well-being. We were in for a treat. This is what it said:

*"Bonnie is extremely caring and kind. She always helps with new, smaller kids. She gets on with everyone and **her presence is missed**. When she was on holiday all the pupils kept asking when she was coming back. She is extremely funny and often makes us laugh".*

The class remembered you because of the way you make them feel, not because of how high you can count or how well you can draw. Everyone has their own strengths that make them special. But what makes a person memorable? My message to you on this very special day is:

People will never forget how you made them feel.

You made a difference at nursery and for that I am bursting with pride. You are flying high, like a little butterfly.

*You will now spend the majority of your day with other people. Those people, be it teachers, carers and friends that you meet along the way are going to have an impact on you. They will all have their own strengths, yet when you are older you will associate names with people. Names many find beautiful may appear ugly. Names you didn't care for before will make you feel all warm and fuzzy. That is down to how those people made you feel. You will forget details along the way but you **will never forget how people made you feel.** The name Bonnie, that first beautiful word you wrote, makes me feel warm and fuzzy. I named your brother, partly, because I will never forget a beautiful, smiley boy I looked after when I worked in America. He had blonde curly hair and a smile that could light up the world. Just like our little, smiley, exceptionally Cheeky Charlie. Some teachers you meet over the years will really make a difference. When I think back to my time at school, there are some teachers that stay with me for all the right reasons. All the things that were in your report. To me – they were perfect for the job. They had an* *impact because they made me feel valued and important. I remember them even after all those years. I have forgotten the finer details but I remember how they made me feel. Even with my absolutely shocking baby brain. Even when I can't remember what I did yesterday when friends or family ask. I still remember them. They still crop up in my mind. They taught me to fly high like a butterfly. They taught me to find strength in me when life gets heavy. They taught me to keep smiling and spreading joy.*

You have made an impact. The class missed you when you were away on holiday because you made them feel good. You have left your little mark at the tender age of four and that blows my mind.

My wish is that you keep that energy and passion that is bursting out of you. You keep that enthusiasm to learn. My wish is that you drown out the wasps and sadly I know you will meet so many. Some days you will be one too. Remind people how to laugh with that amazing sense of humour of yours. Melt hearts with that kind and caring nature. Continue to be someone people don't forget.

*There are days you will feel angry, afraid and sad. Know that those feelings are normal. Know that even the most memorable people get them. Never be ashamed of those feelings, those struggles. Talk about them. Ask for help. Find a passion that helps to heal your soul. I can highly recommend running, writing, cooking and music. I can also recommend having a few cocktails and going out dancing with people that love you. But that is your choice. **Be you.***

There will be people that sting you like a wasp along the way. People that buzz and nip in your ear and try to change you. That makes me so sad. One day you will understand that the greatest happiness comes from loving yourself. It is the longest relationship you will have on this earth. If you learn to be happy with yourself, you will love harder too.

Right now, your favourite song is One Direction – 'What Makes You Beautiful'. To me it is exactly what your nursery report said. It is your quirky, funny and caring nature. Because you could be the easiest on the eye person in the world. You could be the most intelligent person. You may go on to make an absolute fortune. But none of it matters if you make people feel sad and you feel sad about yourself. Be a butterfly, not a wasp that stings and nips in people's heads.

Sometimes as your Mum I get it so wrong. Some days you are so full of excitement, often you shout YES to life and I am one of the wasps. The noise can all get a bit much. I miss moments because I am rushing. Then I feel terrible. How amazing that you have so much energy to go out and enjoy this life?! Thanks for the days you remind me how to stop and laugh. Thanks for the days you are so caring and kind, they light me up. Keep making a difference.

Never stop saying yes to life. When I say this, I don't mean saying yes to ice cream, chocolate and banoffee pie if someone offers you it. Although a tip – if there are a few puddings up for grabs it's always good to go tapas style and try a small bit of everything.

I'm talking about acceptance. I'm talking about saying yes when life makes you sad.

I'm talking about when someone breaks your heart – pull an Adele and create some magic that helps to heal others and inject a little mojo.

I'm also talking about the dreaded D word, when you lose someone you love. Bonnie, at the tender age of five you have said to me on a few occasions:

"Mummy, I want us to die together".

That is the feeling of such pure, unconditional love you have for me at such a young age.

Sadly, losing people we love is a part of life. As is having our hearts broken. As is the ability to get hurt by people we love. Some relationships can get so hard.

But there is something I want you to know. It can be so easy to play the victim. Sometimes things happen. We get our heart broken from the sting of unrequited love. We lose someone we love. We don't get the job we applied for. We get knock backs. Our kids get older and more independent and we have to learn to let them go to an extent. Sometimes we have to accept things and say yes. Say yes with a grateful heart and you will feel so much lighter. Today I say yes to goodbye.

Goodbye my baby. Today, you started school. Fly high my little butterfly.

Mummy JoJo x

A guy called Gav inspired some of the words in this chapter. I heard him give a keynote in 2016 and it blew me away. In his best-selling book, Shine – Rediscovering your energy, happiness and purpose, Gav dubs himself as having a 'palpable sense of ordinariness'. I have to disagree.

I was having coffee with him earlier this year, getting some tips on public speaking to the masses and listening to stories about his already fascinating life. Gav has never been on Love Island (confession I don't watch it and no I don't have FOMO), he doesn't have millions of followers (yet) – phew or I may never have got to have that coffee with him. Yes, he is only human. Yes, he isn't perfect, I am sure the guy has flaws. But one thing I am certain of is that Gav is unforgettable for all the right reasons. He is a person who is impossible to forget. In fact, if you are lucky enough to hear him talk I will give you £50 if you think he sucks. I'm Scottish – that is a lot of money.

Gav shares my passion to motivate people and spread positivity. He encourages us to embrace our freak. He challenges us to be less 'people pleaser' and more what I like to call 'team 100%'. We shall get to clarity in chapter 6. Clarity is very important, yet so often we are afraid to seek it.

Many words stick with us, many we forget. Thanks Gav for using your talent as a writer and keynote speaker to hit hard what really matters. I am proud to know you.

http://gavinoattes.com/

TOOLKIT

Some days you just need to get through the hours. Breathe. Take three huge, deep breaths and enjoy some calm time. Even if there are tears flooding down your face. Even if you are full of rage. Breathing is extremely powerful, but so often we forget to do it properly. I did a breathing test at the Edinburgh Wellbeing festival, which I was hosting this year, and it was so interesting to see how much our breathing impacts our heart rate. I wore a heart monitor and the results were powerful. It is so healthy for our mind and heart to take time to breathe.

Remember that thoughts are just energy. We all get dark, sad, scary, happy, interesting, deep, challenging thoughts. It is OK to feel anger, sadness and fear. These feelings are not permanent. They will pass. These feelings are normal and nothing to be ashamed of. Sometimes you might not be able to pinpoint the reason behind the negative or scary thoughts. Accept them and let them in. But remember that it is possible to feel anger and still be kind. It just takes a bit of an effort. We are only one thought away from turning our day around. For more interesting studies on the power of our thoughts, I would suggest you look into the work of the Scottish legend Sydney Banks.

Stress is not a competition, and everyone is entitled to the dark, scary feelings. Mental wellness does not discriminate and every single one of us experiences stress. We need so much more kindness.

Gratitude is an amazing tool to use once you move into acceptance. Get yourself a beautiful notebook. Write down one thing to be grateful for every single day. Even if it is simply that you are grateful you made it out of bed on a tough day. There is so much to be grateful for in the world, despite how bleak it can sometimes seem. It's not a coincidence that those with the least often find the most to be grateful for.

Saying goodbye is a part of life. Know that it is OK to cry. It is healthy. Know that it is important to grieve.

Allow yourself to feel pain but tell yourself that you deserve the chance to enjoy living again. One bad experience does not have to define you.

Self-care is so underrated – make time for it. Where is your happy place? In the bath with a book, swimming in the sea, going for a run, writing, giving back to others, knitting? Do it as often as you can!

Get the support you need. Sometimes that is a GP, a therapist or life coach. It may take a while to find one and then it clicks. Or find the tribe of people you need. There will be millions of people in the same boat. Find a likeminded support network for people going through the same journey. Be that issues such as parenting, heartbreak, grief, addiction or abuse.

There are a lot of positive people out there that really care. It can be easy to focus on the negative but there are so many incredible people who want to spread a little joy and start talking openly to break the stigma of mental health. Find your community.

I feel incredibly honoured that so many have felt able to share their battles with me. For one, seeing the weight lift from their shoulders as they opened up was beautiful and of course heart-breaking at the same time. I want to share one of them with you, using my words and their confidential words in the form of a letter.

Dear my 5-year-old self,

I want you to know that what just happened is not your fault. I'm so sorry you had to go through that. I am so sorry for all the evil and wrong in this world. You are so beautiful, so full of confidence and love. He has just taken that away from you for a while. He so wrongly took that spark and that passion. For now, he has sapped you of energy. You are not invincible and you need time.

Please NEVER FORGET that you are in no way responsible for what just happened. You are not naughty. You will not get into trouble. I wish you would just tell someone. Please stop feeling ashamed or guilty. I know you are too young to understand this. Too young to understand that you should never ever feel shame. You need and you deserve support, love and help to try and comprehend the extent of what has just happened. You must be so confused right now. You are just a sweet, innocent and precious child. One day you will be able to finally understand you were not to blame. You are a victim right now but this in no way, shape or form has to define you. You are so much more than this. One day you will be able to take all the hurt, take all the anger and let it go. You will be able to focus your incredible energy on all the positive things in your life. You will work hard to encourage children to share their worries with adults.

I promise you this - you have an incredible future ahead. You will make so many in-credible friends. You will build your own family. A family that love you more than you will ever know. You are fun, beautiful, clever and talented. You are going to love to travel and enjoy life. You will sing and dance and touch people in so many wonderful ways with your talents and caring nature. You will NOT be defined by what has just happened. You are broken and fragile just now but you will get through this. You are so strong. You are beautiful, inside and out. You are going to go on and do amazing things. I will be so proud of you.

Anon

CHAPTER 3

BACK OFF 'PERFECT' MUM

"One of the basic rules of the universe is that nothing is perfect. Perfection simply doesn't exist. Without imperfection, neither you nor I would exist".
Stephen Hawking

February 2015

Dear JoJo,

What has happened to you? Since you had Charlie you have got seriously lazy. Are you ok?

I never see you bake scones and craft like some of your friends do. The closest Bonnie gets to crafting these days is when you go to pizza express and they give her those crayons and hats. Stop moaning about the pizza slicers and get on with it. That's the way it is now, restaurants think it is cool to make people cut their own pizza. It's genius.

You need to throw yourself into the Mummy lifestyle with open arms, the beautiful, the fun, exhausting and ugly. Keep calm and carry on. People do not need to hear it. Stop airing your dirty laundry across the internet will you please? It's embarrassing. People aren't interested in your attempt to leave the house with young kids or thoughts on cooking dinner with Charlie pulling and screaming at your feet.

You need to try and keep up the pace. Last week you were in your PJs until 11am! What a disgrace. I don't give a rat's ass if it was raining and you were shattered from Charlie being up most of the night teething. Nor do I care if Bonnie jumped on your head at 6am, just as you fell back to sleep. You need a routine OK? Leaving the house with kids is only stressful because you lazed around too long, staring at your cold cups of tea. Your timekeeping is slipping too, that has always been your strength. Oh, and I saw you get desperate last week when you were trying to fasten Charlie into the car seat. You left him in a dirty nappy. This is just cruel and weird. I don't care if you were going to miss your appointment.

The kids need more fresh air. Get them out to the park, pack some healthy snacks whilst you are at it. You are failing those kids as you sit watching Peter Rabbit, eating chocolate Hobnobs. Last week I heard you on the phone, telling your hubs you didn't want to breastfeed Charlie in a 'baltic play park'. That is not on. The kids need to come first. You do need to work on your feeding skills though, it is not graceful.

I am convinced the kids think you are boring. You need to make them laugh more, it is the medicine of life – be funny! Put your phone down now and do the animal impressions again. Bark like a dog, they like it when you do that.

Don't get me started on your screen addiction. You need to chill out on social media and those work emails. You should be on the floor with the kids playing. Why give your work so much priority over your kids? You should really just quit and adjust your lifestyle accordingly. I bet they think you love your career more than them. What a shame for those beautiful kids, they are such a blessing.

As for drinking on the plane when you were away on your family holiday. Other Mums were judging you for saying, "make mine a double". I don't care if Charlie had just thrown up all over you nor do I care about the fact you are a nervous flyer. You are a Mum now and that means you need to start acting like it. Bye, bye booze buzz and hello healthy lifestyle.

On holiday you put Bonnie into kid's club **most days** and lay and read your book. What decent Mum reads two whole books on holiday? What decent wife does either? If you had to abandon your child, the very least you could have done was service your husband as Charlie napped.

Bonnie's friends have a social life that Katie Price would be envious of. Get more play dates in the diary whilst you are at it. You are slipping on that one BIG style since you had Charlie.

As for their nutrition, stop dishing out pesto pasta yet again from the jar! How lazy have you got? You have changed. Homemade salmon fish fingers would be a nice start, with a **homemade** kale pesto. The kids need to learn table manners. Stop allowing Charlie to throw peas at your face. It's time you brought up important topics such as world peace and kids in Africa. They need to learn how fortunate they are.

I'm also rather shocked that you go to the gym two or three nights a week! After your husband has been working all day long. You expect him to be left to cope with the bedtime routine? You are a housewife. Start taking that role seriously. Stop with the content creation. I don't care if it is a passion. I don't care if it keeps you awake at night with excitement. Stop being so ridiculous. You are a dreamer. **Less dreaming – more cleaning.** *More ironing, cooking and hoovering. I'm telling you now, if you don't listen to me then this marriage won't last long.*

Regards,

Perfect Mum

It's Sunday afternoon and we have been invited over to Morningside, in the South side of Edinburgh, to have coffee with my friend Sophie and her family. They have a beautiful house - a stone's throw away from my favourite artisan cheese shop - IJ Mellis, which sells the best Camembert I have ever tasted. Don't get me started on their Spanish goat's cheese.

I love the South side of town. It has so many fun memories. Hubs and I used to live in a top floor flat; it had a perfect view of Edinburgh Castle from the roof. We put a couple of plant pots and sun loungers up there. It was great for partying the night away followed by some naked sunbathing, weather permitting. Until another neighbour a few doors along found out about it. That was awkward.

We did some serious entertaining in that flat before we had kids. We love a dinner party and I have to be frank: we were bloody amazing at them. What a performance we put on, we were just totally winging it though. So often friends said we "made it look effortless". No way was it effortless. We had them fooled big style.

So much thought went into every single detail, I'm surprised Gregg Wallace and John Torode weren't knocking at our door given the reputation we had in Edinburgh.

What our friends didn't realise is the nightmare lead up to those 'effortless dinner parties'. Hubs was like a dog in heat and it did my head in. The house would have to be spotless. The thought of people seeing a messy house would give him a coronary. Compared to him I am lazy when it comes to keeping the house like a show home. I'm the dreamer, he is the cleaner. It kind of works in a weird way though as I excel in ways he doesn't - timekeeping, organisation and making things happen. I am not a fan of all talk no action. They say opposites attract (although if I had my way he would be less of a nag, more flexible and spontaneous). I digress.

The duster would have had a good seeing to, the carpets hoovered and waxed (Dyson style) and the shelves would be sparklier than Victoria Beckham's engagement ring. The food clearly home cooked and delicious. I always did my research and planned the menu with precision according to our guests. I laugh remembering the day our friends with a foodie level we marked ten out of ten were on the invite list. Best up our game from last weekend's lasagne. I had spent three hours that Saturday afternoon touring Edinburgh in search for foie gras, not even Harvey Nicks stocked it. Yes, I know it is taboo which makes it uncool. Not for a 10/10 foodie though, they don't think that way.

Ironically, I finally found some around the corner on Morningside Road. Yes, I really do love the South side of town with its little boutique shops and quirky coffee houses. Sods law my favourite wine shop, Woodwinters, is that side of town too. It doesn't just sell beautiful wine either. They sell a bottle of fizz that tastes identical to Bollinger for half the price.

All that was fantastic but after five years of Saturday night dinner parties and Sunday morning lying in bed (or naked on the roof) I was overtaken with a desire to start trying for a baby. My husband didn't stand a chance. The first month we agreed to "see what happens" I had the ovulation sticks at the ready. The day I got the 'heads up' I jumped his bones as soon as he got home. The following day I was working at an event in Glasgow from 8am till 11pm. I still jumped his bones when I got home. I would then grab a magazine and lie with my legs in the air for thirty minutes to give those swimmers the best chance (a few friends have thanked me for this tip and I may share it in more detail on a podcast soon). The odds were on our side.

A couple of weeks later and I still remember the shock on my husband's face the moment I rudely interrupted his weekend long lie by rustling around looking for a pregnancy test. I knew the answer before I even did it. We had been out for dinner the night before with friends and my boobs had been aching. That day our lives changed forever. In a really crazy, wonderful way.

I was once the hostess with the most-ess for friends and then our little people stole the show. My placenta clearly kept up to my hosting standard's, dishing out fillet steak and champagne as both our babes were fifteen days late.

I daydream of precious memories of when we had our first baby, little Bonnie Violet. OK, not so little at fifteen days over, ouch, ouch I can still feel those 9lbs 6.5oz – yes, the .5 counts. I used to love walking about this neck of the woods as a new Mum in the baby moon period. Our party pad had hit the dust though and it was time for a new adventure.

We moved to North Edinburgh with its slightly more modest prices (and I mean slightly - this is Edinburgh we are talking about) to a new family house. Corstorphine is a lovely little village not far from the airport, next to Edinburgh Zoo which I have grown to love. The only problem is that the artisan delights aren't exactly on tap. Why does the word 'artisan' make everything sound cool? I'm from a smarmy sales background so I suck it up like Radio 1 with a new Ed Sheeran track.

As we drive over I am a little intimidated. Sophie is a perfectionist. I feel like my high hosting standards seriously slipped after we had the kids. Those horrible 'perfect Mum' thoughts in my head keep telling me this. Hers, no way. She is the Mum that many secretly hate. She had the perfect labour. In the water, five minutes of pushing and gas and air only, of course. All baby weight was gone after a day, as for stretch marks - zero. I went through five bottles of bio oil but it made absolutely no difference.

Sophie is the Mum who can afford a house in the South side of Edinburgh. She is the Mum that looks like she is on route to a Vogue photoshoot. I am Bridget Jones and Sophie is Bridget Bardot. Sophie gets her coffee in her local chic artisan coffee house whilst I grab a Costa. Mental note – must support smaller, local businesses.

She answers the door and I am instantly stunned, how is it even possible to look that good with two young kids?! Perfect Mum tells me it is because her girls sit quietly and draw or read of course unlike our crazy little 'into everything' people. Sophie gets time to do her hair and makeup. She also had time to do a 10k that morning around Arthur's Seat. Perfect Mum calls me a lazy chocolate Hobnob-eating slob.

The place is immaculate. Toys are neatly stacked away out of sight. My little hubby will approve. So will perfect Mum. Finn, her husband, will have had 'the pep talk'. It works well though; he is laid back and obliging. He knows by now to keep the drinks topped up high. I can smell the candles she has on show. She loves The White Company scented ones, Seychelles will be in the hallway. As for the downstairs toilet, ESPA all the way so the place smells like an exotic spa. I am already slightly nervous about the thought of Cheeky Charlie pulling them down and dribbling hot wax all over himself. He is so likely to trash the place. Thankfully he is very cute. It's a dry afternoon so my mission is to get him out into the garden quicker than Donald Trump can update his twitter account.

The kitchen smells amazing. Soph is whipping up some scones. Standard behaviour around here. How on earth does she find the time? I tell her I am WELL impressed and that she *"makes this whole Mum thing look effortless"*.

I am slightly in awe, I mean is she not busy enough? I feel very grateful, but she really didn't have to go to all that effort. I am sitting next to Mother Earth and I feel intimidated. I am a lazy Mum who buys things in packets that are quick and easy. What has happened to me? I lay on the sofa for two hours this morning snuggling whilst she was nailing a new 10k personal best with her new Garmin watch. Perfect Mum tells me that I should be more like Sophie. I wish she would just shut up.

Two Weeks Later

After we went to Sophie's I had a word with perfect Mum. It was a cold, wet morning and Bonnie had drawn all over the chairs and then blamed it on little Charlie. She was caught green felt tip pen handed. I decided I would give this baking thing a shot, I would be perfect Mum and get my apron out Sophie-style. What did I have to lose? It might save our little Picasso from letting loose on further household objects.

Actually, it turns out that making scones was a total success. It was also a great way of keeping the kids quiet and occupied for a good twenty minutes. They had been seriously playing up that day and making scones provided some serious light relief and distraction. Honestly, my kids are like a dog with a bone when they get an idea in their heads. They are SO determined and will go on and on until I cave. The thing is, I apparently drove my parents crazy by being exactly the same. We really do reap what we sow.

Why did I make such a big deal of the baking thing? I love the fact that making scones is so basic: flour and butter, a bit sugar, a bit milk and a bit vanilla essence to sweeten them up. I am getting better each time we make them; practice makes perfect and all that. Some days we go for some grated cheese and sun-dried tomatoes if I want to kill two birds with one stone and cover Bonnie's entertainment and her pre-nursery lunch. Let's face it, anything to keep the dishes down. That is the only difficult thing about baking scones, the dishes. I don't know anyone who actually enjoys doing the dishes. One of my current pet hates is trying to do them as Charlie pulls on my legs wanting picked up.

We had friends round recently and as I whacked a batch of scones in the oven I heard that same familiar line:

"Wow you are making this whole Mum thing look effortless".

They will leave my house feeling like shit, thinking I am perfect Mum if I am not careful. Don't get me wrong – who doesn't love a compliment? It is lovely to have friends say such nice things. I had to be honest though and replied, "letting Bonnie make scones was the only way I could enjoy a cup of tea in peace, because being a Mum is rarely effortless where little people are concerned".

Nothing in life is effortless, by all means use these expressions to flatter and charm people but never believe that effort is effortless.

Hi JoJo,

Thanks for coming around the other week. You always cheer me up. I wish you would stop being so hard on yourself. Bonnie and Charlie are so kind and lovely. You are doing a great job. I love how you always try to be so upbeat and positive.

I have to be honest, you think I make this all look effortless but having two kids is the hardest job I have ever had. I am pretty frazzled these days, so I am sorry if I seemed off the other day. I feel like some days I have nothing left to give.

I want to be the best Mum I can be. You know me, I am a perfectionist. Last week I was smug and made a kale pesto with salmon fishfingers. No doubt you saw me putting it on Instagram. Cooking is so hard with kids screaming at your feet. So is cleaning.

I feel like I have taken on too much and I need to slow down a bit. I need to give the kids time to get bored. Time to use their imagination. My Mother in Law has been encouraging me to book up all the kids classes and activities under the sun. I feel like a glorified taxi driver. I lost it last week when she came over. She keeps trying to help with the housework, but I can't seem to handle anyone trying to help. I like the way I do things. But I know I need to take a break and let people help me. I constantly feel anxious and like I am losing my mind.

Drinks soon?

Soph x

*Note – Sophie is not a real person, but she is based on countless messages I get about people trying to be the most perfect Mum. We are all just winging it and doing our best. My letter from perfect Mum is based on genuine thoughts I have in my head. So glad I am learning to ignore them. For one, I make a great scone when I put my mind to it and if I had spent more time cleaning and less dreaming – there is NO WAY I would have had time to write this book.

"Mummy JoJo, Thank you for this. It is so meaningful to me right now. I keep putting so much pressure on myself to try to be perfect at work because we just started working from home and I don't want them to think I'm sitting here slacking (reading blogs hahahahaha), also I'm behind on laundry, concerned that the meals I'm making don't have enough fresh fruits and vegetables, my brother is coming to see my new place for the first time so it has to be perfect, and on and on and on. I feel like I'm driving myself crazy and end up in tears at least once a day because it's so hard to measure up. But you are so right, I need to just chill. It's all okay. And once I make myself a list of the most important tasks to get done, even if I don't get them all done, I start to feel better as I check them off one by one. Whew! You were my break today. Thank you for such a timely, meaningful post!"

"This is brilliant. Thank you. I so needed it after a rubbish week with all three kids plus hubby being ill so all off usual school / childcare/ work arrangements. "Perfect" mum has been in my ear a lot about there being too little playing, fresh air & discipline and too much TV and iPad viewing & rubbish food. I've felt like I haven't been there for any of them as much as I should have been, despite being here the whole time, as my patience and energy levels have been totally worn down. This post reminds me that the most important thing is that we've just about made it through the week in one piece and that everyone knows I love them. Thanks for keeping it real. Love your blog x"

TOOLKIT

If you are a parent or carer who is prone to getting stressed, feeling guilty and comparing yourself to others, then know you are not alone. Let me repeat that. *You are not alone.* The chances are that you need a mojo injection.

Perhaps like Sophie, you struggle to pass control over because you like the way you do things. Perhaps you can't relax until the house is spotless. Know that this is not always possible, especially with young kids, and sometimes you need to put your mental health first. Sometimes you need to ask for help or accept help when it is offered.

Always prioritise time to do something you enjoy. If you are a single parent then join a support group of likeminded people. Time on your own is so important, as is quality time with the kids.

Talk about the struggles you face, be honest. It will be so reassuring to know that others struggle too. Even if everything looks perfect on the surface. We all have our own issues and critical thoughts that go on.

Try not to take things too seriously. Have a laugh with the kids, get messy every now and again.

Don't fill your diary with too much. Allow time to chill at home, on the sofa. Often the most stressful part of being a parent or carer is trying to leave the house.

NEVER feel guilty for turning on Netflix and passing the kids an iPad or tablet. There are moments that this is essential. It is an absolute Godsend when you need to get other stuff done.

A brisk walk or a run outside may do you the world of good, even if you feel shattered. Running helped me with patience and it gave me essential head space after a long day at home with two young kids. The days can feel very long but of course the years are short. This gave me comfort on the really challenging days.

Phones are extremely addictive. Whilst social media can be a tremendous support, ensure you get time away from the screen. Endlessly scrolling through newsfeeds, especially last thing at night is not good for your mental health. It's all about balance.

Don't be intimidated by parents who make scones. It's not that hard. Never feel guilty about buying them either.

Never assume people with a bigger house (or tidier) are happier. We all have our own issues and our own priorities too. Live the life you want and STOP comparing. You are fine just the way you are. Embrace it.

Comparisons are a waste of time. We all hear that perfect Mum voice of guilt. We all want to do the best job because of course we love these little people unconditionally. But that starts with loving ourselves. Perhaps you love your job and are excited to get back to work. Or you may feel so much happier at home. Don't feel guilty about that, we are all different. I assumed I wanted to be a stay at home Mum that stopped work for fifteen years, like my Mum.

But I am a different person to my amazing Mum and that is OK. We are both wonderful in our own way and so are you. There is no competition. Stop thinking it is. We are all just winging it and doing our best. What matters more than anything is that we find the balance that works for us. Be kind to yourself, you are doing a wonderful job. Your little people love you for the tiny things.

CHAPTER 4
RUN FREE

"He said, 'One day you'll leave this world behind
So live a life you will remember'.
My father told me when I was just a child
These are the nights that never die"
Avicii

Jan 2013

Hubs,

I don't know how you do it. You seem to have so much more determination than I do. Do you actually enjoy exercising? You always have so much energy too.

You work out a lot. It annoys me a bit if I am being honest. It's like you are addicted to the gym and always have to be on the go. I also get annoyed seeing you check yourself out in the mirror. Yes - you look great. You have a hot body and with a tan, wow it is a pretty sight. Come on though - it's a bit self-obsessed is it not?

I am just not meant to be sporty. It doesn't interest me enough and I don't have enough commitment and energy. I am a foodie, are foodies not meant to be a little overweight? I wish you would just join me for the ride. It would make me feel better if we were on the same wave.

I know you hate seeing me get upset in the changing rooms when nothing hangs right. I hate getting ready. I buy clothes I don't like that much. Clothes that cover my lumps and bumps. I have to learn to accept who I am though, this is the way I was made.

JoJo x

February 2015

It's a cold but bright sky-blue February morning. I find Mondays so hard. Hubs is back at work and the kids love to climb the walls. By 9am Charlie had already jumped in the shower with me and needed a change of clothes. He also made several attempts at eating the toilet brush.

Bonnie had a meltdown as hubs had moved the toaster setting and the corner of her toast was burnt. It was a disaster. She was devastated. How could I be so thoughtless as to present her with peanut butter and BURNT toast?! They say burnt toast causes cancer. Oh no. MUST DO BETTER. Perfect Mum had a good winge in my ear that morning.

Going from a two adult to two child ratio, to being outnumbered by these little people, can be daunting. Bonnie hit the nail on the head as we were getting packed up to leave the house:

"Mummy, wouldn't it be great if you had more hands?". Go figure.

Leaving the house with young kids puts me in a head spin. As we are getting packed up, I am frantically searching everywhere for my phone. Then I realise that I am talking on it to hubs, asking if he has seen Bonnie's new welly boots. The joy of baby brain.

We head out to Ravelston play-park, in a lovely leafy district which is close to many of the private schools in Edinburgh. It's a lovely area for a house stalk, we just love drooling over nice houses. Especially ones close to lovely parks. Bonnie starts chatting to another kid on the swings. Naturally I start chatting to her Mum. She is the sporty-looking, 'fit mummy' type. Slim, stylish with thick blonde hair. I am instantly a little intimidated. Why can't I get my shizzle together and bag myself a body like her? I am well jel. I bet hubs would be checking her out if he was here with me.

I can tell she is a runner, she just has **that** look about her. I want to pick her brain as I have just reluctantly signed up for my first ever 10k event in attempt to shift some of my baby weight and get that runners glow everyone talks about. The distance scares me though.

I am an organiser and a planner. I want to know what I have let myself in for. How long is it going to take me to run it? Fit Mum is cooing over Charlie, which is also her favourite boys name. He is still so teeny, all wrapped up snug in his snow suit. I tell her I have just started running and ask if she has ever taken part in any running events. Surprise, surprise – of course she has.

She tells me that I should be careful, she was physically sick at the end of her last 10k event. Oh no, what have I done? I am afraid. If this fit Mama was sick then what are my chances? She shows me some of her running apps on her iPhone and talks me though her latest routes. I am a newbie and I am afraid. That's it – when I get home I will contact The Edinburgh Marathon Festival to switch to the 5k event.

Something stopped me. Yes, I was terrified, but what if I pushed the feelings of fear and doubt aside? Why not give it a try, I mean what's the worst that could happen? How amazing if I proved myself wrong and got the medal? For one, what a story to tell the kids one day. They say it's great to break our comfort zones.

I put in the time and I did the training. I ran in the rain, the hail, after sleepless nights with my hungry little Charlie. I ran when I was tired, I ran when I couldn't be bothered. I kept buying Nike gear because those three simple words got me through some days. **Just do it**. Even with thoughts screaming:

"Whip that bra off girl and hit the sofa".

This thing called running really did give me a glow. People started commenting "wow, you have lost so much weight" and "wow, you are glowing". What they didn't know was that these compliments were just the icing on the cake. I had the exercise buzz, those all-natural, feel-good endorphins are simply magical. I knew I was onto a good thing. I was running for my soul first and then the new dress. Because I know that a strong girl in a sexy dress with no smile is a waste. I wanted both. Running was helping to heal my pain from missing my Dad. It gave me space to remember the good times. The times he would laugh with me and tell me I was his world.

Of course, there were days I couldn't be bothered. That is human nature. As soon as I got into my stride though I was in my happy place. My mind felt calm. Running helped me on the days I struggled to be a Mum or a wife. Running became a treat, all for me.

In no time Charlie was six months old and I was up early to give the distance a shot. My fingers were crossed that the only spew that day would be from my greedy little milk muncher.

My friend Katie came to collect me and we headed out towards Arthur's Seat with large knots in our stomachs. We even arrived an hour before to ensure there was time to use the portable toilets – with all the runner nerves, those queues can get crazy. It takes me back to T in the Park 2001. I was so desperate for a pee that I had to beg people in the mammoth queue to let me skip to the front as I had a 'bladder problem'. I had no kids then so now feel guilty for the poor Mums I skipped past. What a little diva I was but it was painful trying to hold it in. I got my karma back the following night as the Killers were headlining. A cup of something warm came flying through the crowds in my direction. It wasn't water, nor was it beer. I digress.

I had everything planned with military precision - my playlist, all the gear, the safety pins for my top. I couldn't plan the weather but it was a beautiful sunny morning. The atmosphere before a running event really is electric. As the gun fired I felt elated. Then once I had completed the first 1k I realised there was 4k to go before a water station. I had just run up a hill and the May heat from the sun was intense. My anxiety about getting through my first ever running event added to the pressure. I had two options - my mind was screaming with those dark thoughts we all get. Thoughts like:

STOP! There is no way you can do this.

Or

You are not strong enough for this, just give up.

I was verging on a full-on panic attack. I felt the pressure and my anxiety came knocking on my door. So many had sponsored me to raise funds for the mental health foundation. I could picture their faces if I let them down. Imagine raising all that money and not making it to the finish line? Thoughts of Perfect Mum start whispering:

"I told you not to do this, this is your fault for attempting a stupid challenge with a young baby".

STOP. I had to tell the critical thoughts to shut up and replace them with positive ones. I had to be firm with my fragile mind. I kept running. Running is a mental battle. I focused on my music and somewhere I found strength. As I ran past the view of Prestonfield House, a gorgeous boutique hotel where we got married, our aisle song came on my playlist. I had a little tear in my eye as I thought of Dad at home, just out of hospital. I remembered the moment we walked down the aisle together to Caledonia. That song will always give me goose pimples. He was so proud and so scared of crying. I was pumping with adrenalin and as he lifted my veil and kissed my head, he left me and handed me over to someone else. The little girl that he pushed on the swings was starting a new family and a new life. Running is magical in that it transports us to another place. Our feet are moving but our minds feel free. I was in my happy zone, running free from anxiety and getting stronger.

Funnily enough, I ran past a lot of 'fit' looking gals that morning. I also ran past 'fit' looking men. People who would once have intimidated me. I ran with extra weight but it didn't matter because I had done the training and I believed I could finish. There was no sickness for me, just a whole bunch of high fiving at the finish line. I picked up my first marathon medal the following summer. I was once terrified of a 10k but that fear took me to places I never thought would be possible. I got the head down, worked hard and made it happen. Some mornings it was tough. I used to get a bit emotional leaving the house for a four-hour training run on my own. I would kiss the kids goodbye and feel a mixture of nerves for what I was about to do and also excitement. It was during those long training runs that I decided to start this book. Do I regret it? No way.

<   Edinburgh Marathon Festival's post   •••

Jojo Fraser a.k.a Mummy Jojo was a prolific blogger in the lead up to the Edinburgh Marathon. Her aim is to help mental health stop being a taboo subject, and to get people talking about it and not being afraid to do so.

Jojo was inspired to start her EMF campaign after watching her Dad become a stranger, after he was diagnosed with severe depression last year. She signed up for the 2015 EMF 10K and this year, took on the full marathon distance.

Jojo was the official starter of the 2016 EMF 10K on Saturday 28th May, and on the Sunday completed 26.2 miles at the Edinburgh Marathon.

Thanks Jojo for sharing your story with us and for being such a brilliant source of inspiration for so many! Well done! See blog here: mummyjojo.com

#emf2016 #edinburghmarathon

Setting ourselves a challenge keeps life exciting. It mixes things up a bit. Exercise also happens to be really good for us. Not just for our physical health, exercise helps to nurture our mental health. This chocolate Hobnob-eating, slave to the sofa found a love for running.

Some days I want to quit but I keep going. Running and exercise in general gives me much needed head space. It keeps me feeling grounded. It releases tension that I am unaware I have.

When I first started out on my running journey, I often compared myself to people who looked a lot fitter. It turns out that what you weigh can mean nothing when it comes to fitness. Having less weight to carry simply makes running easier.

It is very easy to make assumptions. Stop. Stop comparing yourself to others and have a little faith. Just because someone looks super fit, it doesn't mean that they are. They might just have more self-control when it comes to chocolate, cheese, wine, carbs – FOOD in general. Good for them. You might be a foodie. I am proud to be one myself. Exercise helps us to have a faster metabolism. Most importantly exercise gives us a glow and it is so good for our emotional well-being. It is great to get off that sofa, we just need a bit of determination. You will never regret a workout. Just do it and watch those eyes start to glow, you might even get your mojo back.

Hubs,

I owe you an apology. For one, I take back what I said about you being self-obsessed. As much as you drive me wild some days, you are caring, thoughtful, and you have a beautiful soul. You also work VERY hard in the gym and like to occasionally admire those pecks.

Why shouldn't you appreciate what you see in the mirror? Hard work pays off, you should be proud. If someone worked hard studying for an exam and got an A they would feel proud of their achievement. What is the difference? Perhaps it used to annoy me when I was less active. The days when I couldn't be bothered exercising. The days when I just didn't get it.

I now understand that you are addicted to the energy you get after a workout. You are also addicted to how good you feel at the end. There really is no such thing as a bad workout. Thanks for encouraging me on the days that I just couldn't be bothered. People used to tell me that I was great the way I was. That I pulled off being slightly heavier. They told me that I was beautiful that way and if I was happy that was all that mattered. The problem was though that I wasn't happy. I know you hated seeing me so upset in the changing rooms when we went shopping. I think we know deep down when we lack confidence and energy. It is our choice what we do with that.

Doing the marathon taught me so much. I will never regret it. I am so glad I decided to go for a run that morning. I am so glad I stuck to it.

You are looking great, you work really hard for that body. I know that exercise has helped you through the dark days too. It has helped you heal your addictions.

I am sorry if I didn't encourage you more and recognise just how hard you work and how fit you are. Thanks for being such an inspiration to get off that sofa. Thanks for encouraging me to be a better role model for our kids. I look at people in their eighties in the gym, they look happy and energised. It really is never too late. I am just glad I get it now. I love you.

JoJo x

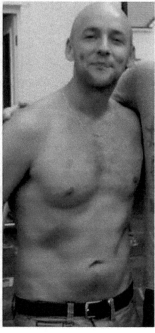

13 likes

proseccomum68 @mummy_jojo_blog after following you for the past 6 months you inspired me to get back into running. Last Sunday I completed my 1st HM. Thank you 💟

mummyjojouncut Awe amazing that is so impressive well done you. Delighted to have helped in some way

"You will never regret going for a run or doing some form of exercise, but you'd regret it if you didn't. Seven weeks post baby number two, number one is eighteen months and I'm ready to start running again. You may just have pushed me to my first attempt! Thanks Mummy JoJo".

TOOLKIT

Feeling fitter and strong offers an incredible and natural mojo injection. We all have our own journey though, and there will be high points and low points.

Like parenthood, don't compare yourself to others. This is your journey, your body and your mind. Don't set goals to compete, set goals to be a better version of yourself.

I exercise because it makes my body feel amazing, it gives me energy, it helps me sleep better, it lifts my mood with a boost of the all-natural happy hormone. It increases my sex drive. It gives me head space and a bit of peace and quiet. Exercise allows me to train for amazing events. It gives me confidence. I never do it to punish myself.

There is nothing wrong with setting new body goals. Feeling stronger is a wonderful thing. But do it for you and nobody else. Because feeling fit helps us to be happier. It releases happy hormones. It gives us confidence.

Find a form of exercise that you enjoy. Do what YOU want to do. Not what others want you to do. Dance, swim, walk in nature, run, lift weights, go horse riding – whatever it is you enjoy. Don't do it because you feel pressure. Perhaps you have tried running and you just don't enjoy it. That is fine. Be you. Find another form of movement that you enjoy. There will be something. Our bodies are made to move. Movement also helps to lower our stress and anxiety levels.

Don't become obsessed with the scales. The scales are sad. I went through a phase of stepping on the scales every Saturday morning. It would make or break my weekend. I had either lost a few pounds (party time), stayed the same (ooops) or put on a pound or two (absolute disaster). Talk about getting into the groove with happy weekend vibes. What a sad way to live. Never mind the glass ceiling, this was the glass circle. A circle I stood on that dictated my self-esteem and my mood. If the number was good I felt proud. If the number was bad I felt like I had failed. Our weight is capable of fluctuating more than the stock market. I chat to people who step on the scales in the morning and then by the time evening comes they are eight pounds heavier.

Use clothes and how you feel in them to measure your progress if you have been advised by a GP to lose or gain some weight. Be aware of how you feel when you are training. Provided you are taking on adequate fuel, you will start to feel stronger and happier from all the natural hormones that keeping active brings.

Always make time to fuel your body and eat good food. This will help to prevent migraines, mood swings and fatigue. Avoid fad diets that make you feel miserable.

Book in a consultation with someone who knows what they are talking about. Surround yourself with positive and inspirational people who will encourage you.

Find a tribe of people who will support you. People who will come running with you or encourage you to hit the gym or keep active.

There are so many mixed messages online. Sometimes it can be hard to know who to trust. Perhaps you love celebrities who promote appetite suppressants. To me that is simply terrifying and SO wrong in so many ways. If you are on social media I would recommend following a guy called Michael Ulloa. He is as straight-talking as they come when it comes to fitness and nutrition and his content is hilarious. This guy is living in his full mojo and it is SO obvious. One thing's for sure – he won't encourage you to do any form of fad dieting. It doesn't work. Stay tuned for some great tips from Michael later on.

I am part of a community in Edinburgh called EGG, set up by the wonderful Kylie Reid, who shares my passion for all things wellness and top artisan coffee (a girl after my own heart). EGG is an extremely powerful and uplifting community of ladies who support each other. Many of them have been an incredible encouragement and have offered me so much support in terms of focus groups and straight-talking about mental wellness.

In this community I met Zoe Macaulay who understands my passion for exercise. Zoe is the Founder of MacFit, which offers outdoor fitness classes for men and woman in Edinburgh.

Zoe and I really bonded over our love of running, mental health stigma-smashing and straight-talking. It was instant people chemistry; deep conversations, and we have become great friends over the past couple of years. She shares her why with me when it comes to exercise.

"Fitness has changed my life in ways that I could never imagine, in just four short years I have gone from being a smoking, drinking party girl to running my own successful fitness business.

I stopped smoking, started running and I signed up for the Edinburgh Half Marathon in 2014 to raise funds for the amazing mental health charity The Joshua Nolan Foundation - a charity set up by my dear friend Laura when she tragically lost her son Josh to suicide. I wanted to get involved to raise funds but also to raise awareness and help break the stigma that surrounds mental health.

Never in a million years did I think that starting my fitness journey back then would have impacted me as much - not only have I, and my children raised thousands for the charity, I found that I LOVED fitness and with the help of a PT I pushed myself in ways that I did not believe possible. Fitness has helped me through the breakdown of my marriage, and the very sudden death of my father. It has helped me be focused, driven and believe in myself, probably for the first time in my life. My mantra in life now is...'Actually I can!'

At the age of 40 I lost my Dad, I ran my first full marathon, I got qualified as a Personal Trainer, started my own business MacFit Edinburgh. Two years down the line business is going from strength to strength, I'm my daughter's hero (this is the best thing to come out of the last four years!) and I can honestly say that I am happier and healthier than I have ever been!

I cannot imagine a life without fitness, the most underused form of natural anti-depressant, and this is only the beginning of my journey..."

CHAPTER 5
SCARS AND PASSION

When the sun will set
Don't you fret
No I have no money on my mind
No money on my mind
Sam Smith

December 2007

Hi Mum,

I hope you won't be too mad. You did raise me to be independent though and I'm twenty-five now BUT I still care what you think. You are my Mum after all. I want you and Dad to be proud of me.

Last night I did something I never thought I would. I went to a place called Haight Ashbury in San Francisco and got a tattoo. I know you can't stand them so let me explain. It's much bigger than I asked him to do it but part of me didn't care. To me it's not really about how it looks. That is not why I got it. I was travelling alone when I had it done. I was nervous and it hurt but I was fine.

I felt compelled to get something written on my body. It's my favourite word. A word that means the world to me: passion. I got it translated into Thai because Thailand was one of my favourite places I have seen this year. It's a place that I had a very important insight about my life. A place I gained clarity, it would be hard not to with those stunning beaches.

You see, before I set off for my year of travelling, I had lost my passion. I lost my passion for what had been an amazing career. It had the potential to go to crazy, exciting places. People in the office commented that my spark, that fire I had, was missing. On top of that, I was in a relationship with someone that felt safe and secure. But something was also missing. I think the real warning sign was outside Edinburgh airport. I couldn't cry when I left him. I got on the flight to Hong Kong with Jen and she asked what on earth was going on. I told her of course I loved him and to stop worrying about me.

Looking back, I now realise that I couldn't cry because something was missing. I needed time to discover exactly who I was. Time to understand what I really wanted in life. He had talked me into cutting my trip down to a few months and going freelance in a career that I wasn't that passionate about. A career that would have more than likely made me a fortune. You often tease me for having extravagant taste but I think you know that money has never been my number one motivation.

The problem is, Mum, that in the past I have let people talk me round too easily. This year I found my passion again. I have found out who I really am. I know that sometimes I need to follow my gut, no matter what advice I get. Some advised me to play it safe. But that didn't fulfil me. My feet were burning. I needed more in my life. I didn't step, I fully jumped out of my comfort zone. I'm so glad I took that flight and travelled the world again. My friends said my life would change forever. Having travelled a lot before I didn't think so.

Last week I was on a boat in Fiji. A guy about your age asked me what I had learned from my year away. I told him everything. I told him everything I am going to tell you when I see you next week. He put his arm around me and said:

"My friend, you have wisdom that money can never buy".

Soon I will fly home to Edinburgh. One thing I discovered this year is that despite my passion for travel, there really is no place like home. My soul is in Edinburgh. I want you to know that I come home happy. I found my passion again. I come home with a tattoo on my arm that you may not like the look of (ooooops). But it's my story and it's something I did for me. It's there for life so I never forget. I will never regret it.

I love you.

JoJo

I stayed true to my word and I came home to Edinburgh buzzing. Friends and family commented on it, my mojo was back.

Everything started falling into place. I got an interview for a sales and marketing job that really excited me. It was like the job had been designed especially for me and I was delighted when the offer came through. Something just clicked.

My role was based in The Bonham Hotel, Edinburgh's first ever boutique hotel which for years was dubbed 'the coolest hotel in the city'. The hotel is located on a beautiful leafy street in the West end of town and I fell in love with it.

The only issue was that I often had to hide my tattoo of choice from clients. Had I owned the hotels, I would have worn it with pride. Boutique hotels are quirky, the whole idea of them is to make a statement through contemporary creativity. I didn't see the problem. For one, entertaining clients on a hot summer evening was hard. I wanted to wear sleeveless dresses. Instead, I would cover my scar of choice with a suit. I get it, though. Because sadly, we still live in a world where we judge people for expressing themselves in a way that is a bit different. We judge people on things like their socks and their hair. What I say is who cares? Let people do what they want. We need to start celebrating the fact that we are all different.

Fast forward the clock ten years and these days I work for myself. I follow my rules and I wear my tattoo with pride. I've just had another three designed on my shoulder based on this book and I adore the art I have chosen for my body. I will never regret it. Even though a few have already commented that they are too big and that tattoos are not a good look. It's my body, it's my choice. It feels so fantastic to write these words. It feels so fantastic to not care about the wasp-like comments. To let them brush over me.

I've gained other scars over the years. Childbirth is an interesting experience. As is growing a baby. I have stretch marks on my legs and stomach. My body has changed.

I found running. I found exercise. It helped me with my confidence. I am amazed by what my body can do. I've lost body fat on my journey with fitness, gained some nice-looking muscle and more importantly I've developed so much mental strength. Exercise will be with me for life and I will continue to shout about its power from the rooftops.

Something I once saw as a chore is an essential part of my week. But I have not lost my scars from growing two amazing babies in my body and I don't care. Bonnie and Charlie have changed me in ways I never thought possible.

I'm cool with my stretch marks. Bonnie and I call them 'magic marks' because she understands that my body made her. My body was her first home. What an incredible vehicle. If I think of it too much it blows my mind. I am a perfectly imperfect Mum and I am so thankful and so proud. The scars on my body are a map of my life. They are part of who I am and they tell such a beautiful story.

When I took part in my eighth running event, which was a half marathon, I had a bad fall. I now have a scar on my leg. I love that scar. The scar reminds me of how I picked myself back up when I fell. It reminds me that I survived those final six miles with blood dripping down my legs. It reminded me that we can pick ourselves back up when life gets a bit heavy. Plus, it made a great selfie, I felt like a rebel.

The scar, as faint as it is, on my stomach reminds me that the hospital was able to cut little Charlie out of me. It reminds me how lucky I am to have a beautiful son. A son who didn't want to come out the natural way. He likes to mix it up and break the rules. A cheeky, incredible little Charlie who will always keep me on my toes.

I spoke earlier of those horrible thoughts I call 'perfect Mum'. Let me ask you, if you were asked to describe her, what would she look like? A few years ago, I would have said she was slim with pert boobs and a tight ass. Her hair would be long and golden, her skin like silk and her makeup flawless. She would wear white and it would stay white all day. That's the media I allowed to fill my head with this image. I did a google search for 'perfect Mum' and got so many images like this. Not a stretch mark in sight. Guess who else came up? Me. This was both a huge shock and a small victory in my mind because it wasn't a glam image. It was simply an image of a Mum trying her best. I hope someone stumbled across that image and felt OK about themselves that day. I believe there is way too much pressure on parents to be perfect. Whatever perfect means.

What about when we are teenagers? As a Mum this terrifies me slightly. I think back to my own childhood. My nickname before I hit puberty was 'pancake girl'. I was very slim with no chest. Then all of a sudden, I was walking around with a huge pair of knockers. It never bothered me that much either way, I just went with the flow. My parents always reminded me that I was beautiful, inside and out.

I was lucky to have very little body confidence issues as I grew up. I was as body positive as they come, I was well ahead of the trend. I danced like nobody was watching. I tried not to compare myself to others. Then slowly but surely, I came into contact with butterflies and wasps. The wasps I met along the way tried to change me. They told me I should lose a bit weight but I was happy and healthy the way I was. I liked being curvy. As I got into the big wide world I had people tell me to hit the gym, to watch what I ate. It made me mad. How dare they. Get out of my face. If I am happy with my body, then leave me alone. The gym wasn't a priority then – my exercise was dancing and walking around the clubs looking for guys. I was young and naïve though and part of me didn't understand that when it came to the wasps, it was their issues and nothing to do with me.

Right now, Bonnie and Charlie are in a magical state. They are too young to care what people think. They are proud of who they are and so proud of me. As we get older, the judgemental voices and perceptions of others that really don't matter, sadly can become part of us.

When I fell pregnant it hit me. There is so much more to life and we are far too hard on ourselves. I never want my kids to hear me shaming my body. No matter what. If it wasn't for my body, they wouldn't be here.

I said, "hello" to my stretch marks. My once pert boobs took a trip South from those little latching mouths but who really cares? It's nothing a good bra can't fix. I am a perfectly imperfect Mum and I am good with that. I could write a long list of what the wasps would say makes me 'imperfect'.

I have laughter lines on my face, I was invited to do a campaign about Botox. Look, I know it's the 'in thing' these days and it can look fab, but for me personally, there are way more important injections to be getting these days. It's all about the mojo. I'm more about the smile and beaming eyes over the lines.

To my kids, in their pure, wonderful minds: I am p
am beautiful. I am flawless. I am their world and my body
created them. Wow. Take a minute to let that sink in. If
you are a parent or carer, do you see yourself through
a child's pure, magical eyes? Or perhaps you are caught
up in the glossy, air brushed magazines full of 'perfect'
people who don't exist 24/7. Perhaps you listen to the
noise. The noise people make about:

"Mums who lost all their baby weight in a day".

Does that make them a better Mum and a better person?

Yes, we can all glam up a little. We can all post beautiful
images across social media. I adore getting my hair and
makeup done and these days I ask for what I like. Give
me a volume blow dry with some smoky eyes and I am
in my element. I feel like a foxy minx. Perhaps for you
it's a part shaved head or long, curly hair extensions. It
doesn't matter as long as it makes you feel good. Some
days feeling good will be forgetting about the hair and
chilling in your onesie and fluffy socks.

When I get ready and my kids say, "you look pretty
Mummy", I say thanks and I smile. Even if my thoughts
tell me otherwise. Those thoughts do not belong in my
mind. They do not belong in yours.

There is so much more to us than the shell of a body we
have. There is so much more to us than our physical and
emotional scars. We have a character, a personality, a

soul. We have habits that make us who we are. Habits that makes us beautiful.

I got picked on by some as I grew up. Sadly, sometimes people become wasps and pick on people for the way they look. This is often a sign that the person has lost their mojo. Why are we all so wrapped up in what other people think of us? Why do we let negative comments pull us away from things that make us happy? We all have insecurities but we have a choice to not let them control us. Once this happens and we start worrying less about the negative comments, our life will 100% change for the better.

Imagine living a life not being phased by the wasps? A life just being caught up in moments. A life where we stayed true to our values. We all have it in us. But looking back there were so many times I let the wasps win. I doubted myself. I listened to them instead of my gut feeling. I focused on the wasps instead of the butterflies who adored me and wanted what was best for me.

Sometimes the butterflies in our life know us more than we know ourselves. Like my friend Colin. He wrote a song for me when I was away from home on that life-changing year. He had been there for some of it early on, having flown out to Thailand in December 2006 for a couple of weeks to show me the ropes. We had a blast and even managed to do some open mic together on the epic Ko San Road. 'Numb' acoustic by Linkin Park was always a firm favourite.

Colin was fully aware of how confused I was before that trip and he watched me fall in love with Thailand and come to life again. As corny as it sounds, I needed time to find myself again. Because sometimes we meet people who steal our identity. I felt like my old self in Thailand. I felt so free and it was so much fun. I laughed a lot too.

I will never forget about nine months later, sitting in an internet café in New Zealand and opening up a file in an email with his beautiful song. The words spoke to me. I knew I had made the right choice to stay for the full year.

The song was called 'The Way you Roll' and the chorus went like this:

Jojo I love the way you roll
You're down for whatever
not trying to be clever
You couldn't care at all
Always yay when its 3 go for a latte with me
The way it should always be
Hey Jo I miss you so
The way we used to roll

Love your scars, they are part of you. Be proud of them. They tell a story of who you are. My first tattoo will ensure I never forget finding myself in Thailand 2006. The three new ones I got this year will ensure I never forget the moment I wrote and shared my first book with you all. Without passion we have no energy. Do things that excite you.

Dear JoJo,

I have been thinking about that email you sent me years ago from San Francisco after you got your tattoo. You know I have never been a fan of them but that doesn't matter. All I want is for you to be happy and healthy. It's your body, be you. That is what matters the most. I've watched you laugh over the years and I have watched you cry. I hated seeing you fall and hurt yourself. I hated seeing you sad. Boys that hurt you and messed you around made me so mad. You got through it. Because when life gets tough we can find a way to cope. We move on and thoughts that are all-consuming feel lighter. The years pass by oh so fast. All those tears and sad feelings fade. We forget the finer details in time.

I remember when you were sixteen. All your lovely school friends went off to get tattoos. You were the only one that didn't because you didn't want one. You were happy to do what you wanted. This shows me that something you learned when you were away really affected you. This shows me that your experience of backpacking around the world had a significant impact on your life. I can understand why you would want to mark that.

I am glad that all these years later you are still glad you did it. For one, I hear they are very painful to remove.

I am so proud that you are now embracing new scars that you can't remove. Because these little grandchildren you have given us are the greatest gift. I am so proud.

Mum (Gran Violet) x

TOOLKIT

We are born perfect but we all have physical or emotional scars which become part of our story and part of who we are.

Try to let people be. Appreciate the fact that we are all different with different stories, but we can all add value.

Take a moment to reflect on your core values. What makes you happy? What feels right to you and your instincts, and what feels wrong. Make a list.

Now write down things that go against your values and try and identify where you can make changes.

Three of my key values are to –

1 – Stay true to things I am passionate about

2 – To raise my kids to be kind and happy

3 – To work hard to find balance in everything I do

This means I avoid jobs that bore me. I do things I want to do, things that interest me and excite me and politely decline things I am not so keen on. I also sometimes have to decline things I want to do because I need to find a bit of balance. I need time to unwind, some weeks I take on too much.

As for the kids, if I want to raise them to be kind and happy then I need to reflect this. I need to speak kindly to myself and my body. I need to speak kindly about my magic marks and show them that I want to look after my body and my mind. I need to speak kindly about others.

Think about some people that make you feel good. What qualities do they have, and do they have the same values that you do?

If someone gives you a compliment, accept it. Don't do the British thing and say, "Awe thanks, I don't feel it". Believe it. Especially if it comes from your kids. Let them know that beauty comes in all different ways.

It can be very easy to get caught up in relationships. Having the same values is really important to get you off to the right track. Hubs and I share our values of a love of family life, sunshine, good music and taking time to slow down. The feeling of freedom is a huge thing for us both. Oh, and champagne, we love it.

Ask yourself what you don't want. What sort of behaviour and activities go against your values? Once you figure this out it will help you to start living the life you love. Proper mojo style.

CHAPTER 6

THE CHAMPAGNE OF THE PARTY

I don't have to sell my soul
He's already in me
I don't need to sell my soul
He's already in me
I wanna be adored
The Stone Roses

February 2008

Hi Robin,

I need your help. I feel like I am either getting let down by men or I end up breaking hearts. I am a fool blinded by lust or love and I turn into a horrible, desperate pushover. I'm that little child in soft play, following the big kids around. Or I watch guys become a pushover for me because they feel that way and I don't have the feelings to give it back. Ah the sting of unrequited love.

I'm getting fed up of it now. All these games. Will I ever settle down? I want to walk down the aisle to my soulmate, I want babies, I want to build a family.

I know we have always been great friends. You are such a good guy. Why are there not more guys out there like you?

Maybe we should have tried? Maybe it could be more than friendship. Or is that weird?

My head is a mess. I love being in a relationship. I love having someone to lie in bed with. I love having someone to snuggle on the sofa with. I love being able to share my secrets, always better when naked. I fixate on a guy's good qualities. I am too trusting. I start planning my future out in my head before I even know them. I am a dreamer. I fall for the idea of who a guy is. How will I know when I have found 'the one'?

Help me please oh wise one.

JoJo x

"My name is JoJo and I wanna be adored". Don't we all?

Thinking back, being a hopeless romantic was exhausting. I was desperate to find my prince. Over the years, I would meet someone and **really** feel something. It could be their eyes, their smile, their banter. It could just be their presence. Sometimes guys would try it on and friends would say:

"He's so hot, why you not keen you weirdo?!".

We are all weird. Let's phase out the word normal. Chemistry is an incredible energy and you can't force it. Looking back, I was searching for a soulmate. I was so hooked on the feeling of falling in love. Those hormones are powerful, what a rush.

The road to finding love can be rocky. It can bruise our ego, it can hurt. There will be some people in life who see you as fine champagne and others a nice but fairly average cava. Some might even see you as a cheap and nasty Lambrini. How rude.

Sometimes you will meet someone you consider a fine champagne who sees you as an average cava, or vice versa. I kept a diary over the years. As I said earlier, I have always been a writer and some of the insights I look back on are powerful. I share with you a few snippets below:

January 1996 (aged 13)

He's just dead cute, with hot, loving eyes. His personality is so warm (cringe, I was a sap and still am).

May 1996

We are going out now. I really enjoyed our first kiss, I didn't know what I was doing and wasn't sure what to expect but it felt nice. I made sure I used my tongue otherwise it wouldn't be a proper kiss would it? Then we held hands. Yes, I have finally lost my V L plates down in Leith (Virgin lips they call it at school).

The sun was definitely shining on Leith that day, Proclaimers style. My heart was not broken.

A few months later

I'm 14 now and I have a new boyfriend. I love spending time with him, I am so happy. Iain doesn't like him though, he is looking out for his wee sister I guess. I heard him in the playground saying, "stay away from my sister". Oooops.

1997

I really like this other guy now. He is two years older and we flirt a lot. He said he likes my eyes. I don't have a clue what is going on but I really want to kiss him as I find him so attractive. I think about him LOADS.

1999

I just got asked to be Head Girl at school! I'm seventeen and it's so bizarre how my life has changed after all these years. I have a great boyfriend, he makes me so happy. I have told him I want to marry him one day.

2000

Should I throw this silly wee book out? I look back and cringe at most of the stuff I have written over the years but at the same time I might regret it in years to come. I'm at Herriot Watt University now which is amazing. I split up with my lovely boyfriend. He is such a nice guy, we had amazing times. I just wasn't ready to settle down. I'm only eighteen.

2001

My nickname at uni is Norway because I can't take my eyes off all these gorgeous Scandinavian men. They are so sexy and such gentleman. The marketing lecturer who loves to crack jokes keeps saying us gals should marry someone from Scandinavia as they are loaded. He might be onto something. One of them told me he was skint last week. I asked how much he had in his account and he looked sad and said, "five thousand". Crazy!

A few months later

He told me I was lucky to be with him, that I am out of his league. He may look like an Abercrombie and Fitch Model but I'm looking for a beautiful soul. I can't believe I was such a pushover.

2002

I'm in a relationship. It's passionate but it's complicated. He's a hard one to read. He loves an adventure. He's creative, smart and gorgeous. He doesn't know it though.

2005

These people actually exist - he said across the dinner table, "When in Rome darling, pipe down and let the men talk more over their brandy". I feel like an idiot. What a sexist asshole. His friends seemed to be enjoying the banter, it was a great night until that point. The worst thing is I cried like a baby and let him speak to me that way. I feel so lonely right now. Why is the world full of such wankers?

November 2006

I have left my amazing job down by the shore, in the media hub of Edinburgh, to travel the world. I've recently got into a relationship though and it has moved pretty fast. I have agreed to cut my trip down from a year to a few months. We have started talking marriage.

December 2006

Oh crap. I have decided to stay for a full year. I'm twenty-four – this might be my last chance for a while. Although staying is going to break his heart. I thought he was 'the one'. The prince that was going to rescue me. I can't believe how my feelings have changed so much.

February 2007

I couldn't seem to find anyone I had chemistry with on the east coast of Australia. A couple of nice guys asked me out but I wasn't feeling it. I should probably take a detox from men for a bit.

A few weeks later

As soon as I saw him dance I was like YES! A man that can move, what a turn on. Good times.

July 2007

Wow! After we went sky diving together I was hooked. I had to kiss him. Then he told me he had a girlfriend and put his fingers to his lips and said, "shhhhhhh this is our secret". REALLY!! Asshole. So sexy though.

November 2007

Last week I had the most amazing couple of days with a guy I met in the hostel. We just connected and talked for hours on end. It felt sad leaving him but I had a flight to catch. He has emailed me already to say he can't get me out of his head. Travelling can be hard when you have to say goodbye to amazing people. I'm in Fiji now and it's stunning but I feel pretty lonely.

January 2008

Baby I tried. I really tried to give you another shot. I thought I could find a way back to you. Losing you is like losing part of me. I love you but I have to love myself more. I choose me now.

Wow, what a roller-coaster, and these are only a few snippets.

We all have our own stories. I wrote a lot of mine down over the years because I have a passion for writing. Writing has always been my mojo injection. There are so many stories I didn't write down. Some people will stay with me, some I will have forgotten along the way. Some made a huge impact, some left me with emotional scars. Some left me thinking I wonder if they had been 'husband material'. It is amazing the impact people we are attracted to can have on us. They can totally consume our thoughts. We want to know more. We want to become part of their life. We crave intimacy with them. We want to know their deepest secrets.

But these intense feelings never last. People can let us down. We can let people down. We are all capable of breaking hearts. Boy I have broken hearts, but I have also been a total pushover. I have let love or lust blind me. I chased, I lost my self-respect. I forgot my self-worth. I blamed myself when things didn't work out. What was wrong with me?

I let people treat me like the shit on their shoes. When I was the champagne of the party, making people laugh and smile, I allowed assholes to tell me to 'tone it down', because a 'city girl like me should sit quietly and let the men talk over their brandy'.

Many will judge 'the champagne of the party' for being over confident. The truth is, even the bubbliest of us are still totally winging this thing called life. Often the champagne of the party will be hiding issues such as anxiety, stress and self-doubt. We judge too easily, which pulls us away from our mojo.

Not everyone will get you. That is OK. There will be people in life that can't stand to see you being the champagne of the party. It is how we react to that which counts.

In the past, I made the wrong choice. I cried. I listened to insults from the wasps instead of rising above it like a butterfly. I was not living in my mojo. I now refuse to allow anyone else's opinions to drag me away from being me.

Neither should you. Have more confidence in yourself. I am a rare, colourful, wonderful butterfly and so are you. We are one of the billions of sperm that attached. We made it. We are a perfectly imperfect miracle.

When we learn to let certain things go, we feel so much lighter. Sometimes you will meet someone you consider a fine champagne who sees you as an average cava. They may always see you that way, no matter what you do. They may even be a complete asshole wasp about it. Because that is their perception of you. Those are their thoughts and they are none of your business. We can't get on and connect with everyone. We may in time be able to change a person's opinions. But chasing after them is such a crazy waste of time. If their perception of you is cava then get focused on your next vintage. Be the champagne of the party. Always be you. Never let anyone change you. Be proud of who you are.

If everyone likes you, the chances are that you are holding back from living in your authentic mojo. You don't have to please everyone. People are going to judge you. It is OK.

I am writing these words as much for myself as I am for you. I am a recovering people pleaser. It was so exhausting.

I have a passion for people but over the years I have lost that balance. I have been working hard to get it back. It's not been easy though because I love my work and the more I share of my life, the more I am opening myself up. The more real I am, the more wasps I am likely to attract. The catch is, that being real makes me happy. Being real also attracts some mind-blowing butterflies. In the past, I held back to please others. This behaviour was detrimental in terms of my growth as a person. Recently I met a beautiful butterfly called Emma Dempsey, who has helped to remind me that I can shift and change. Emma reached out to me after following my stories on Instagram. We met for a coffee and she instantly challenged me and got me thinking about the way I live my life.

There is something incredibly valuable about taking the time to know ourselves and to think about what it is we want from our very short and potentially amazing time here and how we can achieve that. This then enables us to drive life and not let it simply drive us. Growth can be scary and challenging and dark but growth in itself can be incredibly beneficial in terms of enabling us to find our best mojo.

Having worked for a long time in social development, Emma spoke with me about the barriers that many have to living their best life. Low income and bad housing can take away our power and our wellbeing. On the other end of the spectrum there are people who appear to have it all; beautiful homes, an abundance of money and a healthy family, yet they are miserable and feel guilty for not feeling happy with all they have.

Emma has worked in wellbeing and development for over twenty years, latterly as a specialist in Public Health. A big part of her work has always been facilitating change in people and communities and enabling others to live to their true potential. She is passionate about empowering individuals to create change themselves.

We have had a lot of deep conversations about my values and about power. We are all affected by limiting beliefs and it's a powerful thing to watch as these are recognised for what they are and then challenged and changed.

We aren't a homogenous group. We are varied and flawed and brilliant. To quote Emma:

"If we don't feel we have the power to change any of this then we simply don't change any of this. Life is busy and often we don't take the time to think about what it is we are doing. We may be restricted by our actual circumstances, but we are more restricted by our beliefs and our thoughts, they bind us and they limit us and they can keep us from doing what we truly want to be doing. These beliefs and these thoughts aren't who we are, and we can shift and change them as we can shift and change ourselves".

Be memorable. Be vulnerable. Be brave. Be passionate. Be kind. Even when people don't like you. No matter what be memorable for making people feel fantastic. Make people laugh. Melt hearts. Inspire them with your mind and your unique thoughts. There are enough wasps out there, we need more butterflies. Butterflies who are willing to fly to new places and grow.

It took me a while to realise something very important which I shall share with you in the next chapter. In April 2008, after receiving this email below, I met the man I was going to marry. The man who would be the father of my two children.

Hi JoJo,

I hate seeing you upset. You deserve an amazing guy. It will happen, I know it will. You are lucky, you have the ability to fall in love so easily.

I'm flattered that you have suggested we give things a try. You are a gorgeous girl, but you know deep down we are better off as friends.

I think what's happening here is that you have finally realised the type of guy you want to be with. You have often been stuck between two types of men. The geek and the bastard. You are a bit of a geek when you want to be, we all are, but I think you need someone in the middle of the scale.

Now I see a difference in you. You are back home from an incredible year away and you are buzzing right now. I predict it won't be long before you find what you are looking for.

Don't just settle though and don't let anyone treat you like crap. Whoever we end up with will be very lucky.

Robin x

TOOLKIT

I asked the lovely Emma to contribute to the toolkit of this chapter. These words are extremely powerful.

JoJo,

You asked me to write something about self-confidence and I've been mulling it over in my mind. It's funny it's not a word I use that much and I'm aware that we might not all have the same idea of what it means. Thinking about it more was interesting (you know I like a good think!). I have always thought of confidence as being sure of stuff, feeling great about trying new things and speaking out, that kind of thing. Yet that felt temporary, something we can dip in and out of. I was concerned that waiting to feel confident might stop us from ever moving forward, and to be honest I was wary about writing about it. So, with this in mind I sought out some clarity. I'm smiling as I write this, as a coach I always say "everything starts with clarity" yet here at my laptop I have just realised that clarity is what I needed!

So here we go, let's start with a definition. I read various ones but I like Psychology today's the best, that it's "a belief in one's self and one's ability to succeed". I shorten it a little to "a belief in one's self". I like this. It resonates with me and links to my passion about enabling ourselves to feel empowered. It feels less about feeling sure about everything all the time, and more about an underlying belief in ourselves, which can help us flourish. With this definition we can still allow ourselves to feel scared or not ready sometimes and that is just being human.

So how do we get to believe in ourselves in this way? You might have guessed a good place to start...

Clarity *(everything starts with clarity).*

Can we truly believe in ourselves without knowing ourselves? Knowing who we are, what drives us, what values we hold sacred, the things we won't compromise on is a really good place to start. It's not necessarily an easy thing and sometimes we go through life never really stopping to think about it at all. But I can tell you from experience that it's always worth it. Take time to know who you are. Question it, discuss it, take time out, read books, write notes, meditate, talk to a great coach. Explore, unpick, grow.

Awareness *(observing our thoughts so they no longer control us)*

Being more conscious is a wonderful thing. We can get there from starting with the clarity bit. Knowing who we are, we can then look at how we are. Why we do the things we do? What triggers us? What would we like to shift? How would we like to think, to feel, to respond. It's said that, thoughts become feelings, become actions become outcomes. So, let's start with the thoughts.

Here's a quick story. A couple of years ago I ran the marathon. I was doing it for a relative lost to suicide. Because of this there was simply no way I wouldn't have done it. And so, I focused and told myself that no matter what I would get across that line. I got across that line.

Sometime later I was about to start my business, I heard my self say things like, I'm no good at business and I'm rubbish with money. Had I said similar during my marathon training, I'm no good at running, I'm rubbish at training, then I would not have done the marathon. It's that simple. I took that lesson and changed my thoughts and now I have a thriving coaching business and work for one of the best coaching schools in the world. Thoughts become feelings, become actions become outcomes. Be aware of what you're thinking and why you are thinking it. Explore, unpick, grow.

Do stuff

Feeling like you have no power to change anything is shitty. I know it and I get it. We could go deep with this and I could write a whole book about power, but sticking to this letter means you'll just need to believe me. We all have power and stepping into it is an amazing thing. We don't need to change who we are or what we do (though we can) but having a sense of power is for want of a better phrase, incredibly powerful. So, allow yourself to see that. Start small if you need to. But do something that you thought you might never do. I work with people all the time around this and it's such a joyous thing to witness, the process of someone stepping into their power is a beautiful thing. It could be as simple as staying at peace when someone is treating you unfairly. We cannot always change external

*circumstances, but we can change how we react to the
This is power in itself.*

Believe

*And we are back to this. The definition of confidence I
chose for the letter. Believe in yourself. Believe in yourself.
Believe in yourself. For anyone reading this, I absolutely
know you can do it.*

Warm wishes

Emma X

You can find more inspirational content from Emma at
www.forthcoaching.com

CHAPTER 7

MY HUSBAND IS NOT MY PRINCE

Well I found a woman, stronger than anyone I know
She shares my dreams, I hope that someday
I'll share her home
I found a love, to carry more than just my secrets
To carry love, to carry children of our own

Ed Sheeran

April 2008

To my future kids (if I am lucky enough to have any),

I've just had the most amazing first date. It was along a leafy lane just outside Calendar, heading out towards Loch Lomond. We walked, we talked, we kissed. The day was perfect. He's a really good guy and he has a beautiful soul. He is so full of energy. I feel like I could tell him anything. They say eyes are the window to the soul and his eyes are the most striking shade of blue.

I am slightly scarred from previous relationships, but this guy has been friends with one of my best friends for years. She says he is a keeper. We all have our own faults and issues but I'm hoping there will be no mega nasty surprises along the way.

I have a strong gut feeling he is going to be the man I marry and start a family with. He is going to give me you, my babies. I hope you are lucky enough to get his eyes. I've been told over the years that mine are nice but his are really quite special.

You are so lucky, I know he will be a wonderful Daddy. I'll try my best too.

Mummy JoJo x

As my Dad said in his Father of the Bride Speech, I **finally** settled for someone. I did it. I walked down the aisle and married an amazing guy who I often refer to as 'hubs'.

I've been with hubs for ten years. I trust him. I married him because, beyond the incredible chemistry between us, he was a person I knew would support, love and respect me. He got me. He has always known who I am. The times I am wild, the times I am calm. He shares a lot of my values and priorities and I knew he would be an amazing Dad.

When we got together I had baggage from other relationships. I came with issues of trust I had picked up along the way. He had his own baggage too, because let's be straight here, we all do. Once we were blessed with kids, it put so much into perspective for me. All those little things that worried me before seemed so irrelevant. We became a family of four. Life changed.

Having babies with hubs was an all-time highlight of my life. The feelings I experienced were off the scale. I remember lying in bed beside him, in our old party pad in Marchmont, when we brought little Bonnie home at two days old. I felt so much love. I just wanted to make love to him all night. Despite the tiredness and the agony I was feeling from the forceps delivery. I was desperate to be one with him. I was so thankful for him being with me every step of the way and helping me to create the most perfect little baby girl. I was 100% content and satisfied with life. There really was no place I would rather be.

I was fully on cloud nine. My eyes may have had dark circles but they were sparkling.

Just over two years later and those feelings of euphoria returned as we brought our beautiful son, Cheeky Charlie home.

I was right. Hubs is an incredible Dad. There are days he has way more patience than me. He is a big kid at heart with bags of energy and he loves playing with the kids. He runs a tight ship. He loves to keep the house looking great. He never stops. He loves to cook. He loves to make memories with his family. He is loyal.

We are different in many ways though and sometimes we clash. He is a control freak. He has days he snaps. He has days that life gets on top of him. Sometimes he is rude. Sometimes he is moody. Sometimes he is unfair. Sometimes he takes me for granted. Sometimes he lacks spontaneity and flexibility and it drives me wild. Because I **really** know him now and I often take him for granted too.

When we started falling in love on that leafy lane, I made up all sorts of stories in my head. Stories based on my own thoughts. Stories of the sort of man I wanted him to be. He did the same. But we are not the same person. We let each other down at times because we think differently. We don't always want to do the same thing. We have different interests. We have flaws. Some days I think, "if only he thought like me". Some days I think, "what if there is better?" Some days I look at other couples and think they look so happy, so perfect. Even though I have no clue what is going on behind closed doors.

I lived my life waiting for my knight in shining armour. Again, I blame the media. All those glossy, fabulous movies I watched as I grew up. I believed that one day I would find my prince. I believed that he would make my life complete.

It's taken me a long time to realise who 'the one' really is. You see, we tell ourselves there is this perfect person out there. A person who will rescue us. A person who will make our life complete. I thought I had found it with hubs. Then ten years later, it hit me.

No single person on this earth can do that for us. No single job can either, or any material thing that we love, such as a house or a car.

At the heart of it all, our happiness lies in our own hands. The most important relationship we can have on this earth is the one with ourselves. It is the longest relationship we will ever be in. If we can get that right, then it will certainly help all the other relationships we have going on.

Often our relationships are hugely down to what is going on in our heads. Those feelings and thoughts that we have. We should never rely on one person to make us happy. We should never become so dependent on someone that we ignore our own passions and dreams. We should always be kind to someone without becoming a pushover. That just leaves us frazzled and resentful. Sometimes we need to speak out. We need to stay true to our values. We need to remember what excites us, what makes our stomach flip.

When I first got with Hubs and had this strong gut feeling he was 'my one', I put him on such a pedestal. He was responsible for my happiness. He would give me the life of my dreams. I got so consumed by all the things he wanted to do, I spent way less time on my own passions. Then a close friend challenged me. She was worried I had lost myself a little. Was I staying true to that word I got inked on my arm? Or was I just focusing on what he was passionate about?

Relationships are amazing. Intimacy is amazing. Making love is amazing. Friendship is amazing. Having someone to share our lives with is amazing. Creating another human with someone takes it to an even deeper level. A level where you feel the need to fight even harder for your love. Because it's no longer just two people. It's a family unit. A unit that is so special. But if we work on ourselves, if we work on improving our own wellbeing, we will have so much more to offer those closest to us.

April 2018

Bonnie and Charlie,

Well that was a quick decade. You are here now. Bonnie, you are five and Charlie, you are three. You are both at the most magical of ages. Living as large as life, bouncing out of bed with beaming, sparkling eyes. It is wonderful to see.

I was right. That man I wrote about, ten years ago, is your Daddy. We got together in April 2008 and in December 2010 he got down on one knee on Christmas Eve, underneath the Christmas tree. I was over the moon. I started planning our wedding almost straight away. I love how much you both adore coming to Prestonfield House with us. It's a beautiful place. Our wedding day was incredible. Part of me wishes you had been there for it. But it was way too wild for that. We will have a big party there one day, when you are old enough to cherish it.

I knew I wanted to settle down and have a family. I knew I wanted to find that special someone and, as Robin predicted, it happened. I don't like to hang around. I have had my heart broken over the years and I have broken hearts. It took me a while to realise the kind of guy I wanted to be with.

*It has taken me even longer to realise something **very** important though. You see, I am not perfect, and neither is Dad. We have our faults. We lose our temper. We say things we don't mean. We take each other for granted.*

Marriage is hard work, especially when you start a family. Life has ups and downs. Both your grandparents have been together for over forty years. They stuck together. They had issues and battles to deal with. Issues with their mental health. Sticking together is not the norm now. Sometimes people find it impossible to stay together. Every relationship is so different and it takes hard work from both sides. Some people are definitely more compatible than others which certainly helps long term. This is another reason you shouldn't rush into things, like this free spirit Mama of yours.

Always remember that your relationship with yourself is the foundation of everything. If you crack that then any other relationships will have a brilliant head start. If you are not connected and emotionally available to yourself, you cannot be connected and emotionally available to others. It's as simple as that.

Always have respect for yourself. Do things you want to do. Make time to enjoy doing things in and out of your relationships.

Falling in love is an incredible feeling but never forget that you are 'the one' who is in charge of your hopes, dreams and goals. Nobody else can do that for you. There is no such thing as a perfect prince or princess.

Marriage is two people who fall in love so easily and then year by year have to learn to grow together, respect each other and put up with each other's weaknesses.

There is no perfect marriage so don't fool yourself into waiting for a knight in shining armour like you see in the movies. Consult Google and it will define perfect as:

"having all the required or desirable elements, qualities, or characteristics; as good as it is possible to be".

That explains why many are still single – to meet a person on this earth who has all of the required elements is impossible. It may be the reason why people want to travel to space so much these days, just in case there could be better.

*I hope you both meet someone who makes you happy, someone who encourages you to be the champagne of the party. I hope you have moments you get a little smug. I have been there. You see, Daddy and I were dubbed at our wedding by Uncle David, another great writer, 'the champagne of the party'. There are moments I think, "**we are nailing this marriage thing**", because life can be full of moments that feel perfect.*

When Daddy and I gushingly said our vows, we promised with our hearts and souls to put each other first. We used to take such good care of each other. I even brought out the 'baby voice' if he was sick –

"Owwwww my little bubba lie down, I will bring you a Lemsip sweetheart. Let me stroke your head and put a hot towel on it".

He was my only baby you see. Until you both arrived.

You pair stole my heart all over again. To be frank, you are both currently so much cuter than we are. Way, way cuter and so clever with it too. You own us. You also happen to be exhausting. By the time a Friday night arrives I am often too tired to pour a gin and tonic never mind jump on Daddy pig and show him a good time.

Marriage is two people travelling through life together despite their flaws and most annoying habits. Two people who love each other but don't always like each other. People who share common ground but also have different interests too. People who need to make time for each other and time for themselves. Marriage is being honest even if the other person doesn't want to hear it. It is taking time to understand the person we chose to spend the rest of our life with instead of judging them. It is two people coming together from different upbringings and ways of doing things. Two people trying to build a new home.

Marriage is working hard to keep the spark alive and the conversation exciting. No matter how hard we try marriage is taking a person for granted because we know them so well. I know Daddy will always trim your nails before I do.

I know that he will wash all the bed sheets on a Saturday morning (ripping them off me as I cling onto them and beg for another ten minutes). He knows he will come home to his dinner on the table and that I will take care of your dentist appointments, thank-you cards, birthday cards and our social calendar. Do we thank each other for this each time? No.

Marriage is bending the truth sometimes and promising to tidy downstairs whilst the other gives you a bath. Marriage is going upstairs to 'put the clothes away' and playing on Facebook. I have never been great at tidying clothes away and it drives Daddy wild.

Marriage is window shopping and admiring other beautiful people (sometimes not very subtly either).

Sometimes marriage gets too hard. Sometimes we change and we can't find a way back to love. Sometimes, it works, and knowing that we have a special nest at home is enough. A nest that has taken time and patience to make.

Marriage is trying our best to stick together through the hard times when running away seems like the easiest option. Marriage is hoping to fall in love all over again when we fall out of it.

Marriage is being happy to lie on separate sofas. It is enjoying simple things like a cup of tea and a biscuit together. It is laughing at each other and with each other. It is picking each other up when we feel down.

Marriage is sharing this wonderful thing called life together and all its moments – perfect, sad, happy, passionate, euphoric, painful, mundane, frustrating, amazing moments. **Marriage is a crazy ride.**

I hope you find love. I hope you are blessed with a family and we are blessed with grandchildren. But always remember, you alone are the one in control of your happiness. My husband, your Daddy is not my prince.

Love always,

Mummy JoJo

"I just celebrated my first wedding anniversary over the weekend and it wasn't as I expected as we were going through a very rough patch at that time :(Things are getting better now, though and this post gives me hope. Thank you for sharing the REAL beauty behind marriage—no matter how 'ugly' it seems sometimes. May your marriage continue to thrive".

"Could I use some of your words about marriage for a reading at my wedding please Mummy JoJo? You have managed to put on paper exactly what I am thinking".

"Mummy JoJo, can you start an afterhours blog or podcast about relationships. I would love that"

What a fab idea x

TOOLKIT

Always make time for your passions, not just what your other half wants to do.

Communication and compromise is key – talk. There will be times someone feels left out or frustrated. Keep talking and listening.

Accept that you won't always agree. Accept that sometimes you won't always like each other. Try and find a hobby you can enjoy together.

Give each other space to be alone and prioritise family time too.

Leave the mobile phones off the dinner table, put them away for an hour a day. Go for a family walk or day out once a week with no technology.

Remember to laugh and turn the music up louder.

Episode One of my podcast talks very openly about marriage. In fact, having listened to it back I do think that hubs of mine might in fact be a prince. His chat on it ain't golden, it's platinum. We talk very openly about the issues we have faced as a couple since we got together. We talk about issues that have almost ripped us apart, such as addiction. We talk about compromise. We talk about couples that sleep in separate beds and how it may not be as it seems. We talk about trust. Let's keep talking.

CHAPTER 8

PIPE DOWN EGO

Love knows no limit to its endurance, no end to its trust, no fading of its hope; it can outlast anything. It is, in fact, the one thing that still stands when all else has fallen.

1 Corinthians 13:7-10

New Testament

October 2011

Hi Jessie,

I see we are no longer friends on Facebook? I'm trying to wrack my brains as to what I might have done for you to unfriend me. I know we have lost touch, but I still think the world of you.

Is it because I didn't 'like' or even 'love' enough of your posts? Or maybe you don't like my posts? I'm sorry if I offended you in some way. I just can't figure out what I have done.

I am sorry I forgot to wish you happy birthday a while back. I was up North with no signal. I am sorry I didn't hit 'love' when you posted you were going to have another baby. I missed those posts because it was a busy week.

It was a lovely surprise when I saw the pictures of you in hospital holding him. He is so gorgeous.

Seeing you on social media every now and again made me smile and remember the days you were in my life. The days before you moved away.

I'm sorry for whatever I have done for you to want to cut all ties. I'm trying not to take it personally and let it bruise my ego. That kind of behaviour can make us act like dickheads. But it does hurt a bit because I think you are awesome.

JoJo x

Do you overthink things? Do you take it personally if a friend fails to reply to your email? Do you get annoyed if someone doesn't like your Facebook post or pictures? Does an unfollow on Instagram fill you with dread? Do you make up stories in your head? It's because they don't like you. You did something wrong. Are you tempted to adapt? To change to please others?

I know this is an issue as one of my most read pieces to date is a blog I wrote a couple of years ago about why people don't like our posts on Facebook. It scares me how many are searching on google about why people don't like their posts across social media. I feel a sense of urgency to do more. Teenagers are crying in their bedrooms about a lack of likes. Facebook has got so political. We are either annoyed that our Mother in Law never 'likes' our posts but she hits the button for everyone else or seriously hacked off that a Facebook friend didn't take the time to send a quick birthday message. Facebook sends us a reminder each day which means if we are online there is simply no excuse.

If we overthink Facebook it can be all too easy to take things personally. I read a status that went something like this:

"No matter how nice your pictures are or how real your quotes are – there are some people who will never hit the like button just because it's you!"

Guess what? Sometimes your gut feeling might be right. We are all different and sometimes people can be too judgemental and hit the unfollow button without thinking about how it will make you feel. People you were once close to. Sometimes factors such as jealously will hold someone off on hitting the like button. Or what if they have simply not seen your post? More often than not people actually aren't that concerned with you. They think way more about themselves. They may just have been busy. They may not use Facebook. They may be going through a pretty tough time, we all have our own issues to deal with. Or perhaps they enjoy seeing posts but they don't like being public with it. That is their choice, we are all different.

No matter what the reason is, we have two options. To handle the rejection with love over resentment and bash on with life, or to play what I like to call 'card asshole'.

As I have mentioned, I used to waste too much time worrying about what people thought about me. I used to be such a people pleaser. In time I have realised that it's important to be nice to people. But sometimes, no matter what you do, for certain people it's never enough. Don't make the mistake I have in the past and hold back to please people. If everyone likes you then the chances are you are not being as real as you could be. Be you. Not everyone will get you or agree with you but guess what? THAT IS TOTALLY OK! Once you realise this I am talking a full-on mojo injection.

Sometimes you meet people that you think the world of. People you think are really quite special and they don't reciprocate these feelings. Beauty is in the eye of the beholder. We can't change that. There is so much freedom in learning to accept it. How much lighter do you feel? When instead of sitting wasting time worrying about what people think, we focus on other more important things. Things that fuel our soul.

This isn't just when it comes to love either. Some of my friendships were built over time. We can't always connect with people right away. I remember starting at Herriot Watt University. With some of my friends, it was instant people chemistry and we are still the closest of friends today. These people have enriched my life. Then there were a couple that instantly found me a bit too 'out there and intense' and I found them a bit cold. Eighteen years later and those friends have also enriched my life and we are still exceptionally close. In fact, the first blog I ever shared on social media in 2007 (on Bebo – the good old days) encouraged one of those friends to start up his own business. He is now a successful entrepreneur. What an incredible honour to have been a small influence in that journey. We never know when our words will have an impact so use them wisely.

Some people need time to get past their initial perceptions. Some people need time to warm to people and figure them out. Sometimes we judge too quickly, too easily. Sadly, it is still a normal part of life. A part of life which pulls us away from our finest mojo.

What about our careers? Have you had knockbacks even when you really believed you were the person for the job? JK Rowling had so much passion and belief in her work and people told her no. She shared her rejection letters on social media. I wonder how she took it. I wonder if she was ever tempted to pack it all in and go back to the classroom. Thank goodness, she didn't. Think of the millions of people those wonderful stories have entertained. I still remember the smile on her face when she spoke to me about her passion for writing. I get it. I have been writing all my life. It becomes part of who you are.

The school where I met JK Rowling, which is called Leith Academy, has a moto – Perseverance. We all need a little perseverance in our lives. Perseverance to keep working hard and chasing our goals and our dreams.

If we really believe we have a talent at something and are prepared to work hard at it, then why let fear hold us back? Often in life we will get rejected. We all have different things that excite us.

Some will look at a piece of fine art and fall in love with it. Others will fail to understand what all the fuss is about. I remember going for an acting exam for Higher drama when I was sixteen and two ladies on the panel gave me full marks – they were convinced I would go onto be an actress. One of them wrote on the score card: blown away. That person was my cheerleader. What an honour to be able to have an impact on someone in such a short space of time. Wow. Then there were those that thought I was good but other people caught their eye.

It comes back to the cava vs champagne. Some will see you as a fine champagne and others will see you as an average cava. It's how we react to it that counts.

Sometimes we can prove those people that think we are average wrong. Do we let determination lead the way or listen to the negative voices and give up?

I remember watching Pop Idol years ago and screaming at the TV.

How could Simon Cowell find Will Young's voice 'average'? What? I was in love with his voice. He didn't let Simon win, despite the fact that at the time he was the successful guy with all the power. He was polite about it but he said, "I don't think you can ever call that performance average". He then went on to win the show out of thousands.

When I started my blog, I was a little nervous. Initially, I held back a bit. I was careful with my words. Then I started to gain more confidence. People started commenting that my words were having an impact. They encouraged me to keep going. One of my regular readers sent me a quote which read:

"If you think you are too small to make a difference, try sleeping with a mosquito".

Every single one of us can make an incredible difference. For the better or worse. That blows my little mind. How exciting is that? Often, we are way too hard on ourselves, we can't see our amazing wings.

Some of my readers suggested I write a book, something I have always wanted to do but fear or excuses of lack of time held me back. It was then that I stopped caring what people thought. Because I knew I had to keep writing from the heart. I knew I was enough. I knew my words and my honesty were making a difference. I knew I was starting to help people look at mental health in a totally different way.

As for the wasps in life that don't warm to us – not our issue. It is all theirs.

How much freedom in those words? **Let it go.** Breathe. Don't waste another second worrying about it. You will never get inside the head of another person. Why should you want to? Your mind is precious enough.

I recently put a vlog out and over sixteen thousand people watched it on Facebook alone. I had no idea who watched it or what they were thinking. But who cares? I was happy with it and, in my opinion, the material was not harming anyone so I am at peace with that. I worked hard at it and I am proud of my work. It is something I would watch and enjoy. I know many will think the same. The ones that don't enjoy it, so what? Let them go out and enjoy other things. Good for them. The world would be so dull if we all liked the same stuff. This world is large, full of talented people. You are one of them. There is no competition because there is only one you. Maybe you prefer wasps to butterflies. In that case, high five for sticking around with me and making it to this chapter.

Be you. Be true to the person you want to be. Drown out the wasps because for every wasp that stings, there will be a beautiful butterfly that loves you.

Take time to work out what you are good at. What skills do you have, what are your strengths? Every single one of us has them. No matter what background we have, how much money we have or what school we went to. We all have something. Don't let the negative thoughts hold you back. Don't let those that fail to see the beauty in you or your talents bruise your ego. Keep going. With effort amazing things will happen. Effort never goes to waste. If only more would learn to say 'SHUT IT EGO' and bash on. Our time on this earth is so very precious and so very short. The days can be long, but the years fly by and they only get faster.

In a world so full of wasps that sting, be one of life's goal digging butterflies. Be remembered as someone who goes out and makes a difference. Because people will forget the small details but they **never forget how you made them feel.** We are all capable of making people feel so low or so high. Be that champagne of the party. The champagne that lights people up. That lifts spirits. The champagne that encourages, that loves. That sees failure as an opportunity to improve and develop. The champagne that gives and expects nothing in return. The champagne that accepts and like Adele writes their own beautiful music.

And don't take things personally, because it really isn't always about you. Drown out the stories in your sweet mind. Stories that hold you back. Stories that destroy your confidence. They are just stories. Go out and make your own ones.

JoJo,

I am so sorry. I took myself off Facebook and social media after going through a fairly tough time. I just couldn't face anyone.

I'm doing better now, and I would love to see you when I am next in Edinburgh if you would like to catch up? It would be lovely to see you. Keep smiling.

Jessie xx

"Wow, Mummy JoJo - what you say about social media is so true. Why do people take things so personally and make up all sorts of stories? I felt a lot better after reading your blogs about social media and trying not to take everything so personally".

"Mummy Jojo, my teenage daughter is a big fan of you and the awareness you are raising about social media and mental health is so important. I hear of kids crying their eyes out over a lack of Instagram likes or an unfollow. I don't see how we can get around all of the issues online but your posts give me a little faith."

TOOLKIT

If you find yourself wasting hours worrying about what people think then you are not alone. Remember that a lack of contact might be absolutely nothing to do with you. Try not to take things personally.

Give people the opportunity, invite them out. Don't be the person who sits waiting for the phone to ring. If you sense a familiar pattern of being ignored then ask if the person you care for is OK. Potentially they are struggling and they need your support, not criticism.

If you are easily upset by a lack of likes on social media, then take a break from it. Social media is fantastic in many ways, but your mental wellness is way more important.

Not everyone will admire us and that is OK. Do you have the balance between confidence and an egoic mind? Too much ego can be responsible for most of our afflictions including having an inferiority complex, prejudices, judging others, manipulation, rage and the need for praise. Sometimes we need to learn how to pipe down.

Remember that the world isn't against us when we think it is. Tell those thoughts in your pretty head to shut up. Give yourself some self-care.

CHAPTER 9

GOAL DIGGERS

But she said, where'd you wanna go?
How much you wanna risk?
I'm not looking for somebody
With some superhuman gifts
Some superhero
Some fairy-tale bliss
Just something I can turn to
Somebody I can kiss
I want something just like this
Coldplay

October 2014

Dear lazy bones,

Part of me loves you and part of me hates you. We all have it in us to be lazy and procrastinate. It feels great at the time. Sometimes I just need to embrace you because we all need a little lazy in our life. Plus, who doesn't love a cosy onesie? I love some cosy sofa time. I love snuggles. I found hygge way before it was in fashion. I get it. I often find myself dreaming about Christmas, my favourite time of the year. I'm that person who gets the Christmas mugs and candles out as soon as Halloween is finished. The tree is up as soon as I can get away with it and I feel sad each year Hubs forces me to take it down. Last year he suggested we take it down on the 27th!!! I mean, does he even know me at all? Lazy, sometimes you smother me. You suck me in and I feel guilty. I feel tired. I feel low. I need to find the right balance. I'm fed up. I am lacking energy and I find myself making the same excuses over and over and over again. I need to make progress now and you are holding me back.

JoJo

I used to be the queen of excuses. I would hear them in my head over and over again. Some common ones *below:*

I'll start the healthy living on Monday – I need that cake now. And that pasta. Sod it, why not just have a full on final blow out then it's a healthy new me. I'm off to buy a cheese hamper, extra wine and then a takeaway later.

I don't have time to write the book, I've got far too much going on.

It's horrible out there, I will go for a run tomorrow.

Here are the simple facts – we can't be perfect at everything. We can't put effort into every single thing. Because life happens. There are routine things we have to get on with.

In 2015, I decided to pick two goals that really excited me. Goals I felt passionate about. Goals that are part of me and my own story. I took time to understand why the goals were really important to me.

My goals were as follows:

1 - Get fit and run a marathon one day.

2 – Set up a company that would make an impact and smash the stigma of mental health.

I don't need to explain why I set up those goals if you have read this far. You will understand why these goals were so important to me and I made them happen.

Planning was essential to make the goals happen. Initially, the thought of getting to the end result of both goals felt so overwhelming. I was absolutely bricking it.

Of course, there were obstacles – some of those being a whole lot of wasps. Some wasps were just looking out for me. How much stress and commitment would it take? Some wasps didn't want me to do well. Some wasps just didn't get it.

But I bashed on because often slow and steady wins the race. I did something every single day to get me closer to my goals. I worked hard to tell the voices of self-doubt to back off. We are all just winging it and we don't always have to feel confident to get the job done. Fear can empower us to do amazing things.

Ask yourself, how long can I spend today getting me closer to my vision? Let the goal consume your thoughts because if it is something you really want then you will be passionate about it. I'm with Roald Dahl, lukewarm is no good. You need to be passionate as in verging on obsessed with it. You need to feel your feet burn so that you don't just step, you fully jump out of comfort zones. That's how we get closer to our goals. By doing everything we can to get closer to them. You will be challenged. You may even lose some friends along the way.

When I started out building Mummy JoJo, with my vision to make a real impact in the field of mental health and wellness, I had two options. There were **so** many excuses in my head.

- I don't have the time, I have two young kids!

- What if people don't like my stuff? I think I need to go and do more courses first.

- Why would brands want to work with me? There are already so many bloggers and writers out there.

- Will I ever have time to watch TV again?

Then I thought to myself – sod it. Sod this. Because I could feel the passion. I could feel it in my bones and I could see the words staring at me from the ink on my arm. So, I focused. I got to work. Whenever I had ANY time without the kids I would be working. As soon as the grandparents came to help me, I was off working. I was chipping away because I had the goal in mind. The goal of turning a passion into something that would make a difference. A goal of doing something that would have a real impact on people's lives. If I got asked to speak at events, I would always say yes. I wanted to get better at public speaking and talk with passion. I wanted to leave a lasting impact.

Of course, there were wasps trying to get in my head who would say things like:

"Come and work with me instead", or "when are you going to get a real job?"

I didn't listen. I kept working hard. I stopped making excuses. I wrote and created content at every chance I got. Slowly but surely my following started growing. People were writing to me daily to say I inspire them. I help them smile. I remind them how to laugh. I have helped to remove stigma of mental health. I have encouraged them to go to the gym and get into exercise. Not just for their bodies but for their minds.

Then amazing brands started approaching me. They loved my work and authentic voice. They could feel my passion and they wanted to work with me. I got invited into companies to go and give inspirational talks. I got the opportunity to be a regular contributor to the Evening News paper and the Press and Journal. With no experience in journalism, my name was in the paper most weeks. I got called in to be on live national TV. Seeing the proud looks on my Mum and Dad's faces as I drove off to the BBC studio was something I will never forget.

I was invited to be the official starter at the Edinburgh Marathon Festival. Magazines wanted to work with me and feature my work. A lady wrote to me to ask if they could read an extract from one of my pieces about relationships at their wedding.

That wasn't luck. That was ignoring the excuses. That was chipping away. That was ignoring the voices that told me I wasn't good enough. That was ignoring the wasps. That was ignoring the voices that said, "just chill on the sofa and watch trashy TV". Now, I'm not against trashy TV. I always take a little time in the day to unwind, be it after a workout in the hot tub and steam room, in bed with a book or tuning into something on the TV. But when there are goals to focus on, a sacrifice needs to me made.

Do I regret it? No chance. Patience, perseverance, and commitment come easily when you love what you do. I worked hard and made it happen. I wanted to let my life be shaped by the decisions I made, not the ones I didn't.

Then there was my attitude to making fitness a priority in my life. My desire to get stronger was high. But often my attitude got in the way. My mind made excuses which had an impact on my behaviour.

No, I won't train today – it is too cold. I am too tired. I can't be bothered. The sofa is calling. Damn I love you lazy bones.

But my attitude changed because I saw results. I felt –

Energised

Happier

Calmer

Stronger

Healthier

Lighter (inside and out)

My beliefs about exercise changed which had an impact on my behaviour and I stopped making excuses. Exercise to me is an essential part of my week, just like brushing my teeth. I always prioritise time for it. At the start of each week, I make a plan to fit it in.

Some weeks life gets in the way. I feel tired or work gets on top of me. Sometimes I dance in stiletto heels and my back aches for days after, the struggle is real. So, I take a few days off. I go out and see friends or I chill at home. But overall, I go. I tell myself each January that I will not be one of the millions who give up. I will still be prioritising exercise, as long as I am healthy and injury free.

At the start of 2017, as I drove to the gym, I could hardly fit in the gigantic car park. Slowly but surely, as the months drifted by, that car park got quieter. But my car was, and is, always there. Because this goal excites me so I stick with it. It has become part of my life and the essence of who I am. I have finally found a balance that works for me.

Those were my two goals. What are yours? Maybe your goal is to be the most amazing housewife. You want to cook great dishes. Tidy like a boss, do loads of activities with the kids. What an amazing thing to do.

Maybe you want to give back and volunteer, but you don't know where to start. Perhaps you want to learn a new language or pass your driving test. What do you really want to achieve? Get focused. Make a plan. Drown out the excuses and the inner critic in you and see what happens. Slow and steady wins the race.

Dear JoJo,

Look, I know you love me. Everyone loves a bit of lazy. People embrace me when they feel flat. Days they have no motivation. Days they doubt. Days they feel like the world is against them.

Too much of me can be bad, though. Because there is an exciting world out there full of opportunity. Yet so many prefer to lie on the sofa instead of bouncing off it and embracing things that excite the hell out of them. Yeah, that word on your arm, you big geek: embracing passions.

You have trained us to be extremely motivated by fitness and by working hard at things you love because you really believe in it. It's a passion that is now part of your life. Some may call it an obsession but I would much rather feel that way than feel lukewarm about it. If you didn't feel that way then we wouldn't have been able to do what we do. I would have smothered you with my lazy and dragged you to the sofa or comfy bed with those silky white sheets you love so much. Yeah, the ones from John Lewis that hubs moaned about the price of.

You are full of potential, but it also takes a lot of courage to realise it.

*You can float through a life created by circumstances, missing day after day, hour after hour clinging onto me. **Or, you can fight for what you believe in and write the greatest story of your life.** Right now, you are making the right choice and goal digging it like a boss.*

Leave a mark in this world. Have a meaningful life, whatever definition it has for you. Go towards it.

Love,

Your lazy bones x

"Mummy JoJo, I have followed you for a few years now and you have been a massive source of inspiration to me over here in Canada. More people need to follow you. Please keep doing what you do, you help more people than you know!"

The moment I surprised this lovely reader of mine when she came to Edinburgh to do some running events this year. Patricia, you are a wonderful person. Thank you for constantly cheering me on in Canada. It was amazing to be a cheerleader for you at the race my running journey began three years ago, The Edinburgh Marathon festival 10k .

TOOLKIT

Write down one or two things below that you really want to achieve. It can be absolutely anything, making goals is fantastic for our mojo.

Understand why the goals are important to you and your own personal values and dreams.

I caught up with my friend, Michael Ulloa, who I spoke of earlier in Chapter Four, Public Figure and Online PT to ask why he thinks some of his clients nail it and others fail it in terms of fitness or weight loss goals. Michael and I have a running joke that there really needs to be a nail emoji. There is a screw but no nails. Shocking! I once sent him the screw thinking it was a nail when he was featured in Men's Health Magazine. I was implying he was nailing it but it in fact looked like he may have been screwing things right up. Michael is on the podcast and gives some great chat so please tune in for some tips you can trust. You can also follow him at www.michaelulloa.com.

Why do some people nail it JoJo? I believe there are three key aspects that dictate success with weight loss/ fitness goals.

1) The biggest reason for failure is that some clients struggle to find their reason 'why'. "I want to lose two stone" is not enough. Why do you really want to lose weight? If you don't have a strong enough reason why you want to change your life, it is too easy to fall off the wagon and throw in the towel completely. So, you want to lose two stone? Why do you want to do it? You want to run and play with your three-year-old daughter without feeling out of breath? You want to be around for a few more years to spend as much time with your grandkids as possible? Find your reason 'why' and you'll have a far greater chance of success.

2) Not creating a support network. Without a support network, you are setting yourself up for failure. Your motivation might be sky high when you start your fitness journey, but there are going to be days where you feel like crap and you want to give up. This is where your support network comes in. They can be a shoulder to cry on or a supportive hand to drag you out of your slump. This can be a family member, friend, online forum, fitness group or personal trainer. Whichever support network you need to succeed, establish it from the beginning.

3) Not necessarily an issue with my clients as I like to set the record straight about such fads from the beginning; but with the absolute garbage being sold to us through social media and B-list celebrities, the process can be the cause of failure. Sometimes a person can have the best willpower and strongest drive in the world, but they are following the wrong processes. Starving yourself on a very low-calorie diet or drinking detox shakes is not a sensible or sustainable way to go about things. It is a matter of time before they revert back to old eating habits.

Well said Michael – I am sending some nail emojis your way (not screws).

Don't overcomplicate things and don't take on too much. Write out a weekly planner and break the goals down, based on how much time you have.

If you really want to see results then stop talking about it and get focused. Slow and steady is always better. Do something every single day to get you closer to that goal. Whatever it may be. It can be easy to become overwhelmed. When I started training for my marathon, I broke it down to a mile at a time and built up to those gruelling 26.2. Yes, the .2 REALLY counts on the day but it was so worth it.

As Michael says, surround yourself with people who will encourage you. People who understand how important the goal is to you.

Drown out the wasps because there will be plenty of people not living in their mojo who judge too easily. Always follow your gut.

Know if you have lost the balance. To meet our goals, we also need a bit of time to rest. A bit of time out, doing other things too so we can recharge and come back stronger.

Don't forget to sleep.

Even though you are going to be busy, make time for a bit of mindfulness, and we will get to that soon.

CHAPTER 10
FIND BALANCE

We're not invincible, we're not invincible, no
We're only people, we're only people
Hey we're not invincible, we're not invincible

Gary Barlow

September 2013

Dear food,

You and I have had a strange relationship over the years. I have loved you for so long. Mum says I always loved you, I tried every part of you. I was never a fussy child. I ate my vegetables, I loved all sorts of flavours. I embraced you.

Yes, I can't survive without you. I can never cut you out. But I have a problem -sometimes you really get under my skin. I just love you. You are pure pleasure. The way you make me feel when you are in my mouth. I get so excited, sometimes I rush and the act is over too fast. Then I come back for more before my brain tells me I have had enough.

I'll be honest, I feel a little out of control at the moment. I saw a photo of me last week and it gave me a huge shock. I think I am in denial. The GP suggested I try and get some weight off. For one, it would help carrying Bonnie around and running after her.

Some days I worry when I am out going places. I worry you won't be there. It's like I need a fix of you all day long. The feeling of being without you makes me angry, edgy and upset. You are part of my day. When I am eating breakfast, I am often thinking about lunch. You consume me. You are a huge part of holidays and social gatherings. I think about you a lot. I think of all the details from your colours to your smell.

The problem is, there are other important things in my life and I need to remember to find my balance. Let's face it, I need you to stay alive. I need you for energy and there is nothing wrong with loving you. But we need to have other things going on too.

JoJo

I use the word balance a lot and I wanted to dedicate a whole chapter to it. Addiction and balance is a massive part of mental health. I have lost my balance with many things over the years. I remember the first time I worked out how to smoke a cigarette. I was twenty-two and on a girl's holiday in Corfu. One night we were at a club with some guys we met from Texas. They all smoked. I decided to give it another try and I properly inhaled for the first time. I loved it and smoked an entire packet that night. I woke the next day feeling dizzy but I was hooked on the feeling and I wanted more. I remember sneaking off to the beach at sunset. I didn't want my best mate Jen to find out, she would be so disappointed. I loved smoking on the beach that night. Those were the days that you could smoke in bars. I went through a phase for a few months after that of really enjoying it. I was a full-on chain smoker. Then one day I decided it wasn't something I wanted to do full time. The honeymoon period was over and I packed it in.

My true vice is food. Food is hard, because unlike cigarettes which are so bad for us, we can't simply quit. Food is good for us. We need to eat to stay alive and healthy. We need fuel. The say highly palatable foods are the most addictive which tend to be those foods rich in sugar, fat and salt. I just love it all. At breakfast, I would often think about what I would eat for lunch. Then at lunch I contemplated dinner. Food is a huge passion. But like everything in life, whilst it is great to have passions, we need to find a healthy balance.

There have been times over the years I have totally lost that balance. I ate way more than my body needed which left me feeling sluggish and lacking energy. I felt out of control. It was so hard to cut down. The food controlled me.

Addiction is a powerful thing. What is your guilty pleasure? What is your vice? Perhaps it is work, gin, social media, exercise. Perhaps you are struggling with balance right now. Guess what? So many of us are.

When we are living with addictions or a lack of balance, we continue to embrace the issue despite negative consequences, such as weight gain, out of control behaviour or damaged relationships. The addiction takes hold of us.

I've spent time exploring my relationship with food and more recently, I took time to understand it. Why have I always struggled to find the balance? Why have I lacked the self-control to remain at a healthy bodyweight I am happy with since I was in my early twenties?

My gut instincts may tell me because I am happy with myself. I like the pleasure of eating food and I feel diets are punishments. I eat when I am happy. I eat with no guilt. I don't count calories. I am carefree. But there is a catch. Stick with me.

I felt I needed to go on a bit of a journey to explore food. Why have I always dubbed myself as the one who will simply always be a little bit overweight? Is it simply a lack of self-control or is it deeper than that? The very month I realised that I was ready for a deeper insight, a message from Iona popped into my inbox. The timing of this was a 'One For Arthur' kind of moment.

Iona Russel is an example of a butterfly who has struggled with her mental health and has somehow found the strength to pick herself back up and do amazing things.

Iona is a clinical hypnotherapist who is also qualified in **Neuro-linguistic programming (**NLP), life coaching and Kinetic Chain Release (KCR). Her core philosophy is that no matter who you are, where you're from or what your personal circumstances, it is possible to reinvent yourself from the inside out and live your BEST life. We all have innate wellbeing, health and happiness within us. Iona has proven her own philosophy having overcome personal struggles with depression, stress and eating issues. She truly believes everyone can get out of their 'funk' and get to a place of fulfilment and the happiness that they dream of - because she has done it.

Iona had been feeling lost, and like something was missing for years, decades even. From the outside it looked like she had it all. She was married, living in Texas, had a supportive husband, her son was happy and doing well in school. She had great friends, had lots of fun and had an incredible job as a child advocate, making a difference to people's lives. Despite this she felt lost, unfulfilled and alone. She was on anti-depressants and over the course of about thirty years had tried various forms of talk therapy. She tried CBT, Psychodynamic, Art Therapy, Transactional Analysis, and everything in-between.

Gradually she got better, and she found her inner peace, personal fulfilment and happiness.

"You know what the answer was all along - and I joke about this and like to say I went to Texas to find myself. That's not the most obvious place you'd think to go. The truth is the answer was there all along, it was ME. It's simple really, I got still, started mediating and started shifting my thoughts and patterns and as a result my behaviours. The thing that really kicked off my mental and physical wellbeing was mediation. Yep, mediation. I joined a wonderful friendly non-denominational group who met once a week and mediated and openly discussed our experiences. I started eating a mostly plant-based diet, only eating whole foods and exercising. My whole outlook was changing... it was happening slowly, but it was very noticeable. My ex-husband called the change in me 'Zen Iona'. I've struggled with depression, lack of confidence, eating disorders and limiting self-beliefs. No one would have guessed I had any of these issues. I came across as fun loving and full of life.

I remember that I was an incredibly angry and depressed teenager, I felt misunderstood, disconnected from my family and isolated. This was how I felt within myself, which continued into adulthood. (I would like to add here that I do have a wonderful family and amazing friends. They were there all along, it was ME that felt lost).

*The 'story' I was living with and having a party with
- literally -all really kicked off at age fourteen with
alcohol, food and drugs – all unhealthy behaviours
that were not giving me the happiness and fulfilment
and belonging that I was craving. It's all very
classic behaviour you might say, but I was trying to find
all the answers outside myself. Trying to find connection,
fulfilment and happiness. Was I willing to change - heck
no! As a teenager I thought the problem was everyone
else (obviously), as an adult I still looked for the
answers outside.*

*My eating issues started with anorexia
(which I failed at because I was hungry)
which progressed into bulimia. Wow I thought I'd found
the answer with this. I was in total 'control' and I was
getting compliments on how great I looked - and this
felt good - but it was acceptance outside myself - I see
that now. I also tried to slit my wrists during the early
adolescence, it was a temporary 'phase' I wasn't really
committed to doing, I was in hindsight screaming out for
'help'. To my friends though I was fun fun FUN! I honestly
think if I'd have known about self-harming I'd have done
that instead. Being a teenager is tough and I am so
relieved that I didn't grow up with social media.*

*I've learnt it's about how we think about the situation
and the feelings and actions that come from this.
As Dr Wayne Dyer says, 'If you change the way you
look at things, the things you look at change'. We
really are only one thought away from an amazing*

day- the choice is yours. I now get that we really are only one thought away from an amazing day- the choice is yours.

We all just want to be happy, it's that simple, but what makes one person happy may not make someone else happy- One size does not fit all- so I do what I do to help people get there easier and quicker than it took me. Based on this uniqueness of what happiness is, I've developed the 'Joy Jigsaw' which helps us to rediscover what has made us happy, what makes us happy and how to find our happiness again - because it's not gone anywhere, it's there hiding behind the clouds like the sun! It's waiting to burst through the clouds of our thoughts, of limiting beliefs, of a lack of confidence or any other issues. Behind all that we are all OK, we really are OK. We just don't think we are.

Iona took some time to really listen to me. We spoke about food. She said my eyes lit up when I talked about it. I explained to her that it felt like time for growth, time to find a better balance. You see, something about my relationship with food just didn't sit right with me. I wanted to dig a little deeper and try and figure out why food can have such a hold on me. We discussed what my best self would be like and I said I would have more control and balance with food. I also said that as a wellness public figure, I would love to be able to feel comfortable in a pair of skinny jeans and a tight top or a bodycon dress and heels on stage. So why have I stopped myself?

Part of me felt that I was worried that I would become really vain if I lost enough weight to fit into those super tight bodycon dresses. Would it be body positive? If so, surely losing weight would be effortless because I would naturally have self-control around food? I mean, so many others make it look effortless. What was different about me? I'm fit, I feel strong, I can run a marathon. If I have self-control to train, why do I lack self-control around food?

After our initial consultation Iona discovered that my love of food represents family, togetherness and fun. We discussed my attitudes and beliefs as I understood them around food so that she could see if there were any obvious imbalances in the positive intention. One thing I couldn't get my head around is the fact I would continue to go for a second or third helping of food even when I knew I was no longer hungry. I expressed no guilt or shame, or feelings of needing comfort. I explained that my mum grew up on rations, so family and food gatherings were celebrations to be enjoyed. Family memories of food are extremely happy times.

I was interested in trying out hypnotherapy because I know it has worked for many and I was intrigued. Hubs felt the pressure to try it when we got together, it helped him to stop smoking. The issue was though that he wasn't ready to stop back then. I think he resented me for it slightly at the time, although looking back he is glad he stopped. He used to smoke Marlboro reds, those things were nasty!

My primary concern after chatting to Iona was that after hypnotherapy I wouldn't enjoy food anymore and everything it represents to me. She explained that the way she works is not about implanting an aversion to food, it's about resetting my own innate healthy wellbeing and attitudes.

To quote Iona –

"We all have an innate inner knowing about what is healthy and appropriate for us, and this can get distorted by external factors, our own thinking and beliefs. Think of the factory restore setting on our phones, when we get to take it back to before all the bugs and updates got in and messed up the functions. During hypnotherapy I take you back to before you got an imbalance or distortion in your thinking to food. Keep in mind that it is fine to love food and, in some

part, here it is fulfilling a positive intention served up as happy, secure, positive family time. We want to work to fulfil that same positive intention without the unwanted behavior of the unnecessary or excess eating".

This was music to my ears. So, I could keep my love of food and be able to control it easily? Wow.

Like myself, Iona is a fan of the work of Syd Banks and 'The 3 Principles'. I attended a three-day course all about Syd and his books and recordings, which remain as a living legacy to so many. Working so closely with Iona this year has taken me back to that three-day mind spa. A time where I felt really at peace. A time that I was challenged to accept my thoughts.

We spoke a lot about our thinking and beliefs which are behind our feelings and behaviors. Traditional methods of food plans and exercise deal with the immediate environment and behaviors. This is what Iona would call surface level stuff, and in her personal opinion and experiences, whilst it is important - it doesn't change our thinking and beliefs, so any change isn't lasting, it's just temporary. Could this be why so many diets fail? Having looked back at my life, I had to agree. I have had great stages of health and then stages I have struggled to find the perfect balance with food. I found my 'why' with exercise and that has been fixed for years. Food is different. Any eating plans I followed were like putting a plaster on the problem and saying there that'll sort it. But the plaster is just a temporary fix, the thinking is still there. When a cloud passes in front of the sun we still know the sun is there and that it hasn't gone away. If we can change the thoughts and beliefs, then that's when we see BIG lasting changes.

We all have different unbalanced or negative beliefs. The good news is that they are largely false beliefs. Hypnotism gave me the opportunity to gain a greater understanding of my belief systems. Almost all negative core beliefs are connected in a broad way with a feeling of 'loss of self-worth' or of 'not being good enough' for whatever reason we may find. Iona believes that the reason that we think we are not good enough is the most powerful route of the problem.

I appeared to have an unbalanced view of food as a way to keep balance and calm in my life when I was ten years old. Which means that subconsciously as an adult I was literally 'eating' food and having those 'extra' helpings when I wasn't actually hungry or needing nourishment to allow me to maintain a sense of calm and balance. You see, when I was ten years old, I created this belief, and this is the belief that we shifted and I released when I was under hypnotherapy. I now trust my adult self to make the appropriate choices for food and to make 'separate' and appropriate decisions on creating calm and balance - which don't involve consuming food.

As Iona said to me:

"Our lives are a reflection of our beliefs- Change the beliefs and you can change your life".

Someone has to want to change and seek the help that suits them. One size does not fit all. Let me ask you, if you can think of an imbalance now in your life – do you want to change? Perhaps you identify with the role that you are in and you don't know who you would be without that role.

The magic happens outside your comfort zone. For me, it was hypnotism. It scared the life out of me. My heart was beating so fast but I was open to it. I was ready to learn and grow. I did. Suddenly having a balance with food feels effortless. It no longer has a hold over me. I eat what I need. I eat when I am hungry. I feel in control. My thoughts and behaviours around food have totally changed. I have got my mojo back.

Eating too much food was not the issue. My issue is what I was thinking before I reached for more. Issues around food aren't always simple. Iona shared with me how she battled with and beat Anorexia and Bulimia. She has had times of over-exercising and constantly checking the scales, times of comparing herself to others, which fed (pardon the pun) her low self-esteem and lack of confidence. Now she is in a good place and it is truly wonderful to see.

By sorting out our beliefs and thoughts, the behaviour will naturally change all by itself, and this is when we can have lasting change around our issues. It becomes effortless effort. But we need to be ready for it. As I said earlier, I think it finally hit me that I do not have to define myself as the person who has no control around food. I do deserve to feel calm. I do deserve to have control and balance. The very best version of me, living in full mojo has this. Can I keep it up? I'll keep you posted. Perhaps there is another full book on this one and to be honest, I am still processing everything. I love food. I am a foodie, there is no doubt about it. Bonnie is a foodie too and I love eating out with her. I don't want to eat just to live. I eat for pleasure. But food does not have to control me. I can find calm and I can find balance in other ways too and so can you.

Hubs used to struggle with gambling. It consumed his thoughts. He bares his soul on Episode One of my podcast and I am so proud of him for being so open and honest about such a dark time.

Gambling, which started as an innocent positive intention of entertainment, gave him a buzz. A buzz that slowly got out of hand. He was in his bubble, the gambling fully controlled him. It put a spell on him and he surrendered. A bit like me back in the day with a plate of cheese and crackers or a buffet cart #nolimit.

It was a scary time and he did it to punish himself. I remember when I realised just how bad it was. I had to leave the office to drive across town and go into the casino and grab him out before he lost absolutely everything. I will never forget the desperate look on his face, as he was fully controlled by the gambling. He would not leave until he had lost everything. He was in too deep and he needed help.

Initially I screwed it up, I judged him. It was down to a lack of understanding. We make assumptions about people. I couldn't get my head round why someone who loves a deal and always encourages me to 'save for a rainy day', could throw their money away. He couldn't understand why I lacked self-control around food when I hated getting ready because my clothes would no longer fit me. The thing is, it is impossible to get into someone else's head. Judging them is probably the worst thing we can do though. As I said before, judge JoJo was not living in her full mojo.

Having other things to focus on has been his cure. Once he became a Dad, he felt an overwhelming urge to want to change. Change has to come from within. Exercise has also been his therapy. He is now in a great place.

Things we enjoy that give us a buzz are great. Drinking, sex, gambling, food, exercise, iPhone use to name a few. But do they control us, or do we control them? When do our vices get dangerous? When do we lose our balance? When do these things we love cause extreme anxiety? When do they pass the point of enjoyment and become danger?

I had my first ever anxiety attack in 2007 and I can remember it so clearly. I was working for a famous jet boating company in New Zealand. It was on the pier on a very sunny day. I was taking photos of families getting ready to go on the boat. All of a sudden, out of nowhere my mind started playing tricks on me. I started overthinking where I was, who I was and I became very afraid. My heart started to beat fast. It was like my mind had taken over and my legs went to complete jelly. I had the full-on fear that I was losing my mind. I had to get away from the situation and fast. I was not in control. Thankfully it passed after about ten minutes.

That night I got chatting to one of the fellow backpackers who I was living with at the time and he told me I had 'burnt myself out'. I had been partying constantly until all hours in the morning and then I would be up after a quick nap to get to work. Slowly this lifestyle was eating away at me. I was drinking a lot of VERY nice wine (New Zealand vineyards are fantastic). I was loving life, carefree with no responsibilities. I thought I was invincible. I underestimated the power of the booze and lack of sleep.

This panic attack was a wakeup call for me. My body needed a rest. After a year of backpacking I flew back home. I got stuck into that dream job in Marketing as an Account Manager at The Bonham and joined a gym. I started getting fit and healthy and my mind was calm.

My job involved various meetings throughout the day with clients. I couldn't understand it, but I started feeling edgy again. What was wrong with me? It was impacting my mood, my confidence and my sleep patterns. I spoke to my Mum about it and the wise owl asked how strong the coffee in the hotels I worked was. Nail on the head – all those double expresso shots were buzzing me out. I limited myself to one or two cups a day and I felt much better. Who would have thought coffee would have such an impact? Caffeine is more powerful than we think. Something I loved was slowly taking control over me.

I have spoken to people who are the same with sugar. It is addictive and it is powerful. The question is: can we control it, or does it control us? Are we becoming too dependent on it? Personally, I know I have pushed my body too far if my mind starts to feel anxious or my sleep patterns change. I know that it's time to nurture it with all the stuff that is good for us. Healthy food, exercise, good sleep and good company. These things help to keep us feeling calm and grounded. As can enjoying food, caffeine, booze and sugar with family and friends.

It's about finding a balance that works for you. It feels amazing to get the mojo back.

Dear JoJo,

You really do love me, don't you? Don't be embarrassed, lots of people do. I am one massive tease and temptation. I smell incredible, often look incredible and people just can't get enough of me. Once they get their hands on me, I am hard to put down.

Time and time again people come back, begging for more. I am often the way to people's hearts and I am also often the star of the show at parties and family events. Don't worry, it is normal.

I will give you a little space, I promise. There is a great big world out there and I have been hogging your attention. I'm sorry.

Think how much you will enjoy me if you save it for when you need me the most.

Love, food x

"Such an on-time post. I hadn't had an anxiety attack since 2009 but lately this month I have caught myself prior to getting ready to have one three times. I can feel the symptoms (chest pain, feeling out of touch, racing heart) and I know it's a combination of caffeine, the extra pressure put on me this year at work, and maintaining my side hustles (blogs). I have decided to go on another indefinite coffee fast. Folks also laugh at me about my need to sleep and take trips out of town so I can recover, but it's so real and I firmly believe in mental health days.

Thanks so much for sharing".

TOOLKIT

Over to the lovely Iona for this one.

As I said in my story I became 'Zen Iona' and the biggest thing that made the biggest difference is Mediation, and Mediation begins with Breathing. Now if you are anything like my teen you'll be saying, well I am breathing, if I wasn't breathing I'd be dead. I'm talking about conscious breathing here. Most of us breathe really shallow, or even hold our breath unconsciously- I certainly did, and still do sometimes.

Top Tip #1- Breathe!

1- Breathe all the way in through your nose and all the way out through your mouth...S..L..O..W..L..Y and purposefully. Lengthening the breath as you go. Filling your lungs and your tummy- we tend to hold our tummies in- so relax your tummy, relax your shoulders and relax your jaw. You can just sit with this if you like and that's good. Do this for up to ten minutes. Even just a minute will be fab! You can also add a visualisation into this. -on the out breath imagine you are blowing a ribbon out from your mouth and you want to keep it afloat out in front of you... this is one I picked up in yoga.

2- Breathe Aloha. This time again inhale through your nose, all the way in and then breath out saying HA... as in Alo-HA & HA-waii. Do this three times. The HA is like a Big purposeful sigh out. This is my favourite breath and just doing this three times certainly helps me. I like to start and

.. ..iediation with this. In fact, just this breath alone is like a mini mediation for me. Try it! This one I did in Hawaii. True Story- I was actually taught it before I went to Hawaii but I did do it there.

3- Breathe and Relax... and let your thoughts be and just float off. OK, by this I mean we all have so many thoughts going on all at once all the time, and then we think that to meditate we can't have thoughts. Well, that's just not easy for me, I'm not that enlightened. So, what I want you to do is not hold on to the thoughts as they pop in.

There are a couple ways to do this -

Sit up nice and tall with your eyes closed, and whenever a thought pops in just let it be and then let if float off, one thing is for sure a new thought will be along shortly. Don't fight it, don't be frustrated that it's there, don't tell yourself not to have a thought (it's like saying don't think about pink elephants... what happens, all you can do is think about pink elephants) and don't interact with it. I know there are a lot of don'ts here, sorry. Go back to not thinking about pink elephants lol. So, what I mean by not interacting with it is let's say you think, "I forgot to buy milk". OK, that may be true, but then you may start thinking, "who forgets to buy milk, why didn't I just remember, I need to remember to buy milk, I'll get it on the way home" etc. You started interacting with it. Just let it go. (Uh oh the frozen song 'Let It Go' just popped into my head. Sorry if it's in yours now too.) Doing this for five to ten minutes a day will really help calm and relax you. I suggest either breathing normally, or you could add in relaxed breathing in through your nose and out through your mouth in a nice chilled smooth natural rhythm. You might choose to focus on your breath.

Another thing you can do with thoughts when they pop in is imagine you have a chalk board in front of you and when the thought appears you can imagine wiping it away with an eraser.

Or you may like to imagine the thought floating by like a cloud. Yes, it's there, but it's passing by...

Top Tip #2- Get Your Music Mojo On

Now that we've got you breathing let's get you dancing. I know JoJo, who sings for so many of us across social media, will love this one.

Play that funky music, any music that makes you feel like dancing and go for it. Yes, you can dance like no one is watching. If you are feeling energetic in the morning you could kick off your day with a dance party in your room. Enjoy this one!

Alternatively you can wake up to a TUNE that kicks your MOJO into gear and think about what you're grateful for, what you appreciate, and what you love about the song you've chosen. For me at the moment I'm waking up with Robbie William (teehee) – 'I Love my Life'. :D

Top Tip #3- Create Your Mojo Mindset List

Fold a piece of paper in half and on one side right all the things you do that you know make you happy. These can be things you've done in the past and things that you do at the moment. Then on the other side of the list write down anything you are curious about trying, anything at all; you can really get creative and think outside the box here. It's something you've never done but you've thought about trying it. Now do something from this list every day, and you can keep adding to this list. It's YOUR Mojo Mindset list! Alternatively, write these down on pieces of paper and put them in a jar and pull one out every day and do it, or plan it (obviously some of your Mojo's might need some planning to get done).

Top Tip #4- What Are Your Thoughts Saying?

Because I've talked so much about thoughts in this chapter. I want you to just start noticing your thoughts. Are they positive or negative, are they empowering or disempowering? Noticing them is the first step. Notice how you feel when you have these thoughts and the behaviour and actions that follow. Do you want to change this pattern? See if you can think of a belief that is attached to this thought. And think is it true, even if it was once true, is it true right now at this moment in time, and how would you feel without that thought. Spend time with this. You might just be able to realise it's not true and you might just let it go.

You really are just one thought away from an a day. Good luck.

You can find free downloads and audios on Iona's website - available to help with breathing, relaxation, mediation and wellbeing – www.*ionarussell.com*

CHAPTER 11

ANXIETY AND PASS THE PARCEL

See, this is an emergency
Nobody's helping me
Somebody get this out of my mind
There's just no urgency
And I'm in agony
Oh, why is no one listening
James Arthur

May 2018

Dear anxiety,

We are all born with you. We all need you to stay alive. But some of us have a little too much of you in our life. Will you please stop being so greedy. Why don't you back off out of my mind and let me get on with living please? I have kids now and I need to ensure I do my best to encourage them to live their best lives.

JoJo

Pass the parcel is a great game. As parents and carers, we have the potential to pass a lot over. Granted, Hubs and I are totally winging it but if I tell the perfect Mum voice to back off, I think we are doing pretty good at this parenting thing. It is clear to see, and people tell us, that the kids have a lovely nature. They are kind and nice to be around. They are currently more butterfly than wasp. But we muck it up sometimes. Bonnie said, "shut it prick" the other day. Those words do not suit her. To be honest I had to laugh, it sounded so unnatural coming from her sweet little mouth. Then she whispered to little Charlie to say it too. She must have heard me shouting at Hubs the other night when he complained about my 'clothes pile chair'. Yip, that chair. That chair that gathers piles of clothes that I need to hang up and put away. There are two camps. The camp that puts the clothes pile away at once, perhaps in colour order like that hubs of mine and the camp that holds the clothes pile a little lower on the priority list. I mean, as JK Rowling said, we are not superhuman and we cannot do it all.

Hubs often moans about my clothes piles and I moan about his timekeeping. You see, as we covered in Chapter 3 – nobody is perfect.

One thing I am desperate not to pass over to the kids is my anxiety. I've completed courses on raising kids with confidence. I have read up on it. I'm trying.

Anxiety is an epidemic and many are hiding it. I have hope that we can rewire our anxious little brains. I also believe that many of us who suffer from anxiety are incredible people with creative intellect. It is not a sign of weakness.

I'm an anxious person and sometimes I struggle with things I can't control. Like taking a flight, getting on a crowded tube, driving on the motorway or simply walking in a park that allows dogs I don't know to run free. These things I can't control sometimes make my stomach flip and my heart beat fast. What if the plane crashes and what if the dog turns psycho like the one when I was seven and bites my arm off? What if a bomb goes off on the tube or I collide with a drunk driver driving down the M8 at seventy miles an hour? These anxious feelings at times surround me but I refuse to let them define me. I am still able to live. I leave the house and do things. I feel the fear and do it anyway. I really want to encourage Bonnie and Charlie to do the same.

We are all born with anxiety. We need it to stay alive. Sometimes people with higher levels of it play it safe. I played it safe for years. My parents must have been delighted. I never drank so much that I passed out and woke up somewhere random, like a park. I refused drugs when friends would go raving on a Saturday night. I would never walk alone in the dark. I kept myself far away from drama and violence.

I can't actually remember the first time I showed symptoms of being anxious. I used to hide behind my parents when someone tried to take my photo. How ironic. At nursery

I cried like a baby when my Mum left me. I got extremely nervous if too much attention was on me at school. I would shake, sometimes uncontrollably.

As I got older, fresh symptoms developed. On the bus if someone came on with a bag I would worry it was a bomb. Angry people scared me. Practical tests scared me. I would shake uncontrollably. I am convinced I passed my driving test because the examiner felt sorry for me. He was meant to be the scary, tough guy too. Throughout the reverse park, I was shaking more than Miley Cyrus's ass in full twerk mode. It was utterly mortifying. That's not me. I can turn on my confident and positive hat. I can make people laugh when I am on stage. I get the job done. I don't let anxiety take hold of me.

One day it hit me that I needed to make changes. I needed to take charge of those anxious thoughts. I needed to nurture my body and find the right balance with my vices.

We have all experienced some form of panic. From the moment we come into the world we are screaming in shock. Anxiety is part of us for a reason, it is there to protect us. However, sometimes it can reach a point that it is holding us back from really living. Perhaps we are so crippled by fear that we stay indoors. We avoid travelling, we avoid crowded areas. We refuse to visit friends who we need to drive to via the motorway. Perhaps an experience will trigger the fear and we need help to move on.

A full-blown anxiety attack is intense, I will never forget that moment on the pier. If you have had one you will understand just how terrifying it can be. The mind is precious and when we feel out of control it can be all too overwhelming. It's important to remember that a panic attack won't kill you, even if you feel like you are dying. An attack includes a combination of the following signs and symptoms:

- Shortness of breath or hyperventilation
- Heart palpitations or a racing heart
- Chest pain or discomfort
- Trembling or shaking
- Choking feeling
- Feeling unreal or detached from your surroundings
- Sweating
- Nausea or upset stomach
- Feeling dizzy, light-headed, or faint
- Numbness or tingling sensations
- Hot or cold flashes
- Fear of dying, losing control or going crazy

Feeling out of control is nothing to be embarrassed about. There is help out there and sometimes we just need to know the warning signs. We need to recognise when the anxious thoughts come knocking and mentally tick them off as anxiety. We need to think about how we can cut back on things that trigger anxiety.

Stress is often linked with anxiety. Stress builds and various pressures in life take hold of us. Work, relationships, expectations and financial commitments are often the top culprits. It's important to remember that we all deal with stress in different ways. Stress can make us an asshole. Stress can make us feel sick or dizzy. We are all fearfully and wonderfully made. If your cup is running on empty then you are more prone to flaring up with anxiety.

These days I work hard to practise self-care so I can be a better Mum. If Bonnie and Charlie see me in a state of anxiety, it can be unsettling for them. Although I often preach about this life not being a performance, the kids look to me for security and I long to give it to them. I long for them to feel safe and secure. There is evidence that children of anxious parents are more likely to exhibit anxiety themselves, a probable combination of genetic risk factors and learned behaviours. A baby is not scared of a spider. A lot of anxiety is learned behaviour. This has given me a massive kick up the butt to make an effort to control my thoughts and behaviours.

I'm constantly thinking of my facial expressions, tone of voice, words and the intensity of the emotion I express, because kids are reading us. They pick up on everything. Talk about pressure.

Guilt is wasted energy though because:

1. It is impossible to constantly suppress our emotions. It's OK—and even healthy—for children to see us cope with stress every now and then. They need to learn that it is okay to not always be okay.

2. There are also a lot of things out of our control. We can't keep our kids wrapped up in cotton wool. It takes a village to raise a child and one single event can trigger anxiety. Many life events are out of our control. A huge one is that we can't control the words that come out of other people. People can say hurtful things.

Being aware of the triggers and symptoms is a great starting point. Anxiety may have a grip on you, but it does not have to define you.

JoJo,

Like food, you need me. I keep you alive. I keep you from crossing a busy street and I keep you from doing anything really stupid. I am there to protect you. But I get it. I'm sorry for the times I told you not to book that flight in case it crashed. You would have had an amazing trip with the girls. I am sorry for the time I told you to stay at home, because driving on the motorway was too dangerous. I'm sorry that I triggered all those horrible stomach pains when a dog ran towards you. That wasn't great when you were training for the marathon and had to keep diverting your routes. I know it made you embarrassed too. Some dog owners took it personally. I'm sorry for the times I kept playing that car crash over and over in your head. I am sorry for the times I flared up when you least expected it. You are not invincible though and you were not nurturing your body and mind like it deserved. You lost the balance and I was trying to tell you to calm down. To drink a bit less, to get a bit more sleep and go easy on the caffeine too.

Now go out and enjoy yourself. I'm still here when you need me.

Anxiety x

TOOLKIT

Sharing really helps. Emma O'Connor, author of 'Everyday Happy', is living proof of this. I have asked her to contribute to the toolkit for this one because she has lived and breathed anxiety. When she was ten years old, she forgot how to be happy. She was worried and anxious about everything. Sadly, she had to watch the same happen to her son, who was too anxious to go to school for some time. With limited support available at the time, Emma felt an urgency to take action.

Emma has been studying the subject of happiness closely and believes that our happiness can be greatly improved by a bunch of small choices. Positive psychologists say that there are certain habits, or specific things you can do each day that will help to keep anxiety at bay and increase the level of happiness. In her journal for happiness, Emma lists these activities.

I have been working through the journal with Bonnie for over a year now and I have found it really useful. I strongly agree with many of the tips that are provided in the journal, and some of them I have covered already in previous chapters. I shall share a few others from Everyday Happy.

Music

We use music a lot at home to calm us down. I have been known to blast out super chilled beats as I cook dinner. It helps. I have also been known to blast The Spice Girls and dance around the kitchen, singing into a wooden spoon. It has helped to make people laugh when they have been feeling anxious which is an amazing thing.

Laughter

When we take ourselves too seriously, issues can build. Laughter is amazing therapy. When was the last time you laughed out loud? If we are not laughing, we are too busy. I can also recommend laughter yoga, and this is something I am planning to try on the podcast soon.

Photos

Taking photos of something beautiful can be extremely therapeutic and it also helps us to take time out, away for our phones and screens, to be grateful for something. The world is beautiful but so often we miss it. Taking time to admire (or even notice) a beautiful tree or flower is really good for us. I live next to a big open green park and so often I miss how impressive it is because I am rushing. Funnily enough, Bonnie can tell me all about the flowers and the colours on the trees.

A diary from Emma O'Connor, author of 'Everyday Happy' - A Journal for Happiness

October 2014

Pacing.... waiting... pacing... waiting... He went in today, it was hard, and heart-breaking and guilt-inducing... but he went in. That's the main thing, right? Now I'm pacing... waiting for a call from the school to tell me he's been sick, left the classroom or run out the gate. No call yet. That's good right? Anxiety has taken our boy away. Our beautiful, bubbly, gregarious, intelligent boy is a mere shadow of his former self. I want him back. He's nine and I can barely get him to leave the house, school makes him physically sick, and forget any form of club. It's all too hard. I'm in a bubble I can't seem to get out of. I'm angry at the school for their inability to help. I'm pissed at my friends for not understanding and saying the wrong things. I'm so sad... I miss him so much. I want him back.

November 2014

Daily life is easier now. It's not life as we knew it. No school, no clubs, no friends. Nowhere without me. I'm suffocating. We can go to the beach though, and the museum, and a cafe... as long as no one tries talking to him... he doesn't like that. I don't have the daily school struggle. There's this guy who talks about happiness. This could be our answer. We have shifted our conversation, talking about gratitude, practicing kindness, noticing the good things in our day. I'm hopeful...

April 2015

They all think he should go back to school. I hate them all. I'm scared.

May 2015

Looking at schools. Still scared. Researching happiness, healing through happiness.

June 2015

We've picked a school... It seems OK

July 2015

He's going to the holiday club at the new school he's going to start in August. I want him to get used to going there, used to the journey, used to the people, feel confident. I'm not confident... They seem nice enough. He is staying, not crying, not feeling sick.

August 2015

School day one, plan one doesn't work... (oh no...) School day two, plan two doesn't work... (breathe) School day three, plan three doesn't work... a random school mum hugs me outside the school. (Thank you) School day four, plan four doesn't work... (£&@?) School day five, plan five works... or starts to work... progress... (phew) The plan is a person. A living human who is there every morning to hand him to. A caring person to gently guide him to class. I'm grateful. This day marked the end of a difficult year, and the beginning of two more difficult years... But there was progress. We were moving up and getting better. Over these two roller coaster years he received counselling, I received counselling, and we all kept learning and practicing tools for happiness at home. Gradually and consistently his confidence grew, to the point where he managed going in on his own with the others, sang in the Christmas concert (I was in bits) and attended P7 camp... a moment I still can't quite believe. Eventually I was kicked out of counselling because I didn't need it anymore.

Now

Bye... Love you... Have a good day... He's off to school. My boy is back.

CHAPTER 12
A LETTER TO MY IPHONE

Meet me in the crowd, people, people
Throw your love around, love me, love me
Take it into town, happy, happy
Put it in the ground where the flowers grow
Gold and silver shine
Shiny happy people holding hands
Shiny happy people holding hands
Shiny happy people laughing

R.E.M

January 2017

Hey, my new best friend. I am loving your banter and your little gold back. You are one slick model. We have a lot of great times. You come crammed with fun, exciting emails and all sorts of fabulousness. I like having you around. In fact, I recently felt pretty lost without you. It was like a part of me was missing. My fingers started twitching and I became grumpy, dazed and confused. It was a case of serious FOMO. Then eighteen hours later I picked you up. I felt complete again. Until my Mum and my friends started asking if I still care. I felt a pang of guilt. Then hubs and I got chatting. Turns out, he is feeling a bit neglected too. As are my kids. I hope they all know I love them so much more than I love you.

Do you know my four-year-old has grown two inches in the past month?! Nah you probably don't care. Look, iPhone, I need to be honest. You may be painted gold but these little people are the cutest, most magical things that have ever happened to me. You should know them pretty well now. You are filled with images of them. Yes, I am sorry it must get pretty boring compared to some of the images you used to get.

It's 2017 now old pal and I am making some changes. I can't really go back on them either as I wrote about them in the news. Lots of people read it and lots of people have written to me about it. It turns out they feel the same and sadly some so much worse.

Smoking, gambling, booze, drugs, coffee and sugar – they are all way last season. It turns out you my little dear are the current problem. Phone addiction is real, and it seems I am not the only one struggling. You make it so hard for me to be present sometimes. Present with people I love. Something needs to give.

I have no intention of throwing you away like I would with a packet of fags or a bottle of vodka. I need you for so many reasons BUT, one thing I know, if I lost you it would be awful. Those eighteen hours were long. But if I lost those I love, those people who are actually breathing, talking, walking – that would be so much worse. They need to know that no matter what I will ALWAYS love them so much more than I will ever love you.

JoJo x

After I published an article in the evening news, back in January 2017, I was inundated with messages. Messages from people really struggling to find the balance with their phones. Messages of people having lost relationships over their phones.

You see, I had left my phone at my brother's house on a Saturday afternoon. I decided I would pick it up the following day and take a bit of a phone detox. It was actually really liberating. As we were going to bed on Saturday night, Hubs commented that he had really enjoyed the night with me. He commented how present I had been and that he missed that. He really enjoyed our conversations. WOW. How is that for a reality check?

Do you ever find yourself just aimlessly staring at your phone? Scrolling, then some more and some more. Scroll, scroll, scroll. You know that deep down it's time to give up. There are other people around. People that would enjoy your conversation. You feel guilty but you can't stop. It's a bit like going for that third helping of food on Christmas Day even though you are screaming, "what am I doing?"

I often feel this way. There are so many lists to get through. People to contact. Did I say happy birthday to those on Facebook I got an update about? Did I like enough photos on Instagram? What if I offend people? I need to make an effort. Don't get me started on all those group chats on WhatsApp. Ah the pressure.

Perhaps you are on the bus and you get a smile from the person next to you. You look up quickly, but that phone is just far too alluring. Or you are walking around and it's a really gorgeous day. The sun is shining, people are brushing past you but you can't bring yourself to look up. The scroll culture is calling.

Often if I am out for a meal and the food is fantastic I need to capture it. Then I notice a few new emails to catch up on. Whilst I am here I may as well load the nutritional value from the meal on My Fitness Pal. Oh crap - WhatsApp is flashing, I better check it. I better check and reply to the group chat. In case all my friends get annoyed. Either way I am going to offend someone.

These little things are so controlling, so addictive. Technology is an incredible thing. If it wasn't for my phone, there is no way I would have been able to achieve some of the massive goals I set for myself. But it was at one point in danger of turning me into a robot.

Does your phone keep you from being present? Mine was starting to have an impact on my closest relationships. The people I love mean so much more to me than a bit of metal and plastic. I started to worry that those special people in my life thought I loved my phone more.

We all need a wakeup call. I am naturally quite a defensive person. How dare people boss me around. Do they have any idea how busy I am? Don't they care? Why can't they just be proud of me? I don't moan at friends or family and make them feel bad if they are on their phone. What gives people the right to moan at me? I am working hard.

But they had a point, as much as I found that hard to admit. It's good to listen. It is healthy to put the phone away for a while. It is healthy and excellent for our wellness to be present. Taking time to stop and be mindful is so good for the soul. Deep down we all know the secrets to happy and healthy relationships. I'm trying harder to be present. So much harder.

I am reaping the benefits of this. You see, being present truly opens up our mind to those 'One For Arthur' spiritual, tear-jerking type moments.

I was recently out for dinner with my friend Claire. Although we had our phones on the table – she has a young baby and I needed to snap some footage for a food and wine review – there was a whole lot of deep talking as we tasted some stunning Spanish wine and tapas. In Corstorphine may I add, a few years later and team artisan is getting stronger.

Some of the things we discussed were seriously mind blowing. Claire told me a very powerful story. Often in life we are so busy on our phones that we miss moments. Moments that can take our breath away. Moments that make us go holy crap! This was one of those moments. I had goose pimples down my whole body.

Many are scared of the word spiritual as it implies we have to be religious. I believe we can all be spiritual. I believe that, when we are too closed minded we miss mind blowing moments. I think of spiritual as part of our soul which is loving and accepting. Accepting that sometimes really bad things happen. Then the world, or God if you believe, gives us a sign and it literally takes our breath away in that moment. It doesn't happen often but when it does it can make us so present that it puts goose pimples all down our body and brings tears to our eyes and the only word we can bring ourselves to mutter is wow. Just wow. A sign that, despite all that pain you have been through, is bittersweet and absolutely beautiful. But often we miss those moments as we are scrolling through our phones.

Dear JoJo,

Thanks for that lovely new cover you got me by the way, it's baltic this winter. Although, do you need to keep all your cards in it? It's getting a little cramped in here. You are right. I'm not fussed with all those pictures of the kids. I mean they are cute but come on! I miss the old images. Perfect Mum will be happy though.

Look, I know you get a bit of slack from your hubs and your Mum. I heard that friend bang on at you last month too for checking work stuff and doing Instagram stories.

Look, I get that I am one amazing device. It's OK, everyone loves me these days. But I think it would do you good to put me away a little bit more. Plus, I get tired too, you know, and pretty damn hot.

Your family and friends need reminded of how much you care. They need time with just you. You have missed some fantastic stories and moments because I often get in the way. It was good to see those tears in your eyes when you spoke last week. It was good to see you present. It was lovely hearing you tell your Mum how much she means to you. Telling her that you think she is wonderful, even when you forget to say it. Telling her how thankful you are for her. For how much she cares and how much she does. Reminding her how very loved she is. I'm quite jealous.

Now, go and let your hair down at your book launch please and fill me up with some cheeky photos. Leave that cocky new camera you got at home, you will have a photographer that day. I'm sick of it banging into me and taking up too much space in your handbags.

iPhone x

"Mummy JoJo, your article spoke to me. I too am addicted to my phone and find myself disengaged from my children a lot and also from reality at times and even though I hate it, I still continue

I couldn't tell you the last time I picked up and read an actual book or the last time I sat and played a board game or Lego or cars for hours with the kids but I do know what's happening on Facebook and who's doing what and where they're drinking champagne or what their Christmas tree looks like. Whilst I say this tongue firmly in cheek - I can also say, quite honestly with a heavy heart that my relationship with my phone is a very unhealthy one. Whilst I will not be giving up my phone or Facebook or Instagram or the rest it will not be such a priority or a big part in my life. I can't actually believe that this situation has even occurred- How did it happen? How did technology take hold?

It's time for me to reconnect with my small people, who are growing so fast in front of me and for me, because it is my job to make them feel important at all times and to find their self-worth. I want to look at them with full concentration every time they speak to me and give them my everything and not just answer them without looking at them because I'm on my phone, it's my job to make them feel valued and worthy before it's too late and they've flown the nest and I've missed it and I've missed them and their special moments and I send them out into the big bad world thinking that it's OK to be disengaged with our surroundings. I am addicted to my

phone and I hate it!
Phones and social media are fabulous but we must find
their place as we lose sight of what's important. Thank
you for your article, as I read it from my phone with
the guilt pangs, it 100% confirmed that I must break
free from my cycle. I hope that I can learn to live in the
present and I hope that I can show up for my kids. I want
them to know how much I love them, whilst my focus is
my phone they cannot know how much.
Thanks again for publicity bringing it home to me and
for being honest that it really made me consider lots of
things today. Thank you, x".

TOOLKIT

Find a hobby you can enjoy tech free. Go to a yoga class or spa and leave your phone in the locker. Get out in the fresh air and leave the phone at home.

If you love photography, then invest in a nice camera instead. You can upload to social media later.

Run a nice hot bath with your favourite oil and substitute the phone for a book.

Leave the phone in another room when you watch a film or read a book.

If you are in company, try and keep the phone off the dinner table. Really listen and focus on being present when you get quality time with those you love. Give them the very best of you. Work hard but love harder.

Try and have a tech free half day or full day a week. I like to do this on a Sunday if possible.

CHAPTER 13

MINDFULNESS WHEN YOU ARE HAPPY BEING BUSY

Today this could be, the greatest day of our lives
Before it all ends, before we run out of time
Stay close to me,
Stay close to me
Watch the world come alive tonight
Stay close to me.

Take That

November 2017

Dear goal digger,

You really are on a mission right now. You showed lazy the front door. I'm loving it. Exciting things are happening. Good times indeed. I love being busy with you. But sometimes it does get a bit overwhelming and I need to learn to take some time out. Whilst goals and plans and dreams are all rosy, I don't want to miss the amazing things that are right in front of me right now.

JoJo x

I have been studying mindfulness for some time. I struggle with it, but I know how essential it is for us. In fact, I think practising mindfulness is going to become a normal part of life. Mindfulness is important but practising it can be harder than getting published. It takes perseverance.

How often do you get lost in your own head? (That's if you are not looking down at your phone.) I get lost in my own head too much. It's like a battle between wanting to embrace moments but also wanting to tick things off mentally. Hubs gets the raw end of the stick sometimes because my head can be scrambled.

I just love being busy. I love setting goals. I love meeting new people. I love an adventure. But *sometimes I find it hard to be present and my hopes and dreams clash BIG STYLE with the mindful magic of my kid*s.

Sometimes their noise levels clash with my writing or creative time. Sometimes I don't want to be on the floor, playing with plastic toys. Sometimes I want to read adult stuff or have an adult conversation. Sometimes our kids just want to be left to watch a film, sometimes they need time to chill out and unwind. Granted the balance will change.

We can't give our kids 100% of our energy, being lost in their beautiful world every second of every day. That doesn't mean that we don't cherish the times we do. It sure doesn't mean I won't continue to write gushy words about the wonder of these little people.

Some days when our kids come running through at 6am, full of zest for life, I need to give them the iPad and cherish my sleep. That is OK. Sleep is very good for us, especially if we were up a little later than planned – working, watching Netflix (#hooked), training, getting jiggy – whatever floats that sweet little boat of yours.

This is the same for our friends and family. Sometimes we can't give them everything because we have lists to get through. Sometimes Hubs will go on and on about his day and my mind is elsewhere. The question is – when does it get to the point that we are missing our share of magic because we are too busy to stop and take it all in?

As I mentioned, I have battled with anxiety for most of my life and since I have started focusing on mindfulness over the past few years, my stress levels have decreased. My anxiety levels are so much lower. I am a nicer, more positive and happy person to be around. Even when the stresses and pressures of being a busy, working Mum can try and pull all the magic and mojo away from me.

I love to be busy but sometimes I need to work on a better balance. Days like Maspie Den, my perfect family day out and hands down one of my top days of 2017.

I started that day with the intention to be present and to be grateful. I had suggested we go to Pitlochry. One of my favourite childhood memories is going there on a day trip. Despite the fact my Dad can't see, he was adamant that Mum would drive us to Queens View. He wanted us to see it so much. Talk about a selfless act, one of the many reasons my Dad is my hero and inspiration.

Hubs discovered a place called Maspie Den instead as he was on the loo hiding on his phone as I embraced the madness of getting two young kids packed up. Cheers Google. Hubs is obsessed with waterfalls and was also craving fish and chips from good old Anstruther fish bar. The best fish and chips I have tasted in Scotland to date. Maspie Den is a magical place less than two hours' drive from Edinburgh, in Fife, with walks and waterfalls and tunnels.

It was a beautiful, crisp Autumn Sunday morning. The perfect opportunity to embrace a family adventure. I put my phone off for most of the day. I got lost in the magic of our little people. I made an effort to quieten my mind.

I was present. I focused on the smell of the woodland walk. I focused on the sound of the waterfalls. I focused on the warmth of Charlie's hand as he wrapped his fingers around mine. I focused on what Bonnie had to tell me. She was filled with stories and jokes. I focused on the steps and the darkness of the little tunnels we walked through. I focused on the fresh air. When the sun started beating down, I focused on how the heat felt on my skin.

I focused on the taste of my coffee, I took my time over it. I enjoyed a slice of homemade ginger cake without gobbling it down. I enjoyed sitting on the beach, eating fish and chips next to Bonnie, with sand in my toes.

We took a slow, chilled sunset drive home along the coastal route and the views were incredible. The kids were singing in the back and at that moment, life felt pretty damn perfect. I was present and at peace with life with no cares and to-do lists. I felt calm.

I often come back to that day. That day was pure mindfully magic at it's very best and it was wonderful. They say we should live each day like it is our last and Maspie Den was one of those days I call 'worthy of a last one'.

Whilst I can't be in the mindset of Maspie Den every day, I like to practise what I call gushy mindfulness and it doesn't take too long.

Although I love being busy and often rush around daft, most days I practise mindfulness by sitting calmly with the kids and focusing on their little faces or their hands. I find early in the morning or last thing at night such a peaceful time. It is the perfect zone for gushy mindfulness. I often crawl into bed with little Charlie and then Bonnie. I take a few minutes to lie and watch the expressions on their sleepy little faces. Sometimes their fingers are locked around mine and they look so beautiful. I stroke their soft cheeks and stare in awe at them. Often in those simple moments I am so present that I get tears in my eyes. Because I am so focused on how magical these little people are. Now, that doesn't mean I don't rush and get stressed at them throughout the day. But I live by quality of moments. Those moments for me are what I call gushy mindfulness at it's very best. Those are the moments we never forget.

What moments are gushy mindfulness for you? Where is your happy place? Where do you feel safe and truly at home? Some of my places –

Snuggled under the duvet or a blanket with my kids or Hubs.

On the beach with the sand beneath my feet.

Walking next to a waterfall and listening to the sound of the water.

Being in the water – such as a hot steamy bath or the sea or a pool with the sun beaming down on my face.

Sitting calmly with a delicious meal, with my phone far away from the table.

Singing and dancing.

Writing something compelling.

Having a meaningful, real conversation with family and friends about things that matter to me.

These are some of my happy, magical places. Places where I feel calm and at peace. Find yours and get gushy. Because mindfulness feels so good.

Part of the reason kids are so magical is because they are so mindful. Mindfulness is hard for those of us that love to be busy but there are ways we can make it realistic.

Namaste x

Dear busy people,

I want to share a few things with you, because I know a lot of you will be feeling like me. You are busy. Perhaps you are busy with a job you love or a project. Perhaps you are busy trying to do things around the house. Maybe you are caring for a sick relative or friend or you just have a lot on your plate.

Parenthood is a roller coaster and it is always busy. Busy getting out the house, busy rushing about to the park or soft play when the kids need to burn off energy. Busy juggling work and parenthood. Busy attempting to tidy up all the crazy mess. Busy being a taxi driver. Busy trying not to freak out about Play-Doh, Lego or paint carnage. Busy trying to rush to the gym or fit in a quick shopping trip.

I want to remind you about my inner critic, 'Perfect' Mum. The busier I am, the more she shows up.

"Your poor kids, they think you don't care about them, you are always too busy — other parents play with their kids way more than you do".

Ouch, that hurt.

When I hear those thoughts, I sit the kids down and say something like:

"I love you both so much. Even when I am rushing around and forget to say it". Then (OK I am desperate), "do you guys love me?"

Their response:

"Of course, we love you Mummy". Phew. 'Perfect' Mum loves to have her say though:

"I bet they would love you way much more if you actually spent more time with them. You are too busy and you are missing these precious years. You will never get them back you know that right?"

AHHHHH SHUT IT. Leave me alone you nasty, horrible voice. I tried but I couldn't ignore it – 'perfect' Mum 1 – Mummy JoJo a big fat 0.

I hear myself mutter to my poor little people:

"What do you love about me?"

Seriously, how needy am I? By this point I had lost Charlie to Paw Patrol and Bonnie looked a bit confused. She then replied:

"I love you when you give me chocolate, take me to school and tickle my back".

It got me thinking. Are we too busy worrying about being too busy? Just because we are often busy, it doesn't mean we can't show love to our kids. We just need to learn to do it quickly some days. I've always been big on quality not quantity.

Gushy mindfulness is powerful. It is sheer quality time in a shot. Sometimes it lasts a full day, like at Maspie Den. Sometimes it lasts a few minutes. It's not a competition.

I know it is hard but try not to waste time with parent guilt. My kids scream, "I love you so much Mummy" *when I serve them their favourite dinner or give them a chocolate bar. They love us for the little things more than we will ever know.*

You are doing a wonderful job, and your kids, family and friends love you. Don't feel guilty if you love being busy.

JoJo x

"Awe this is just needed was feeling mummy guilt as my six-year-old has started saying I miss you so much even when you're next to me and I only work two days. But today she said you're the best most beautiful mummy in the world.
I think we stress too much they just need to know they are loved and they're happy x".

"Having been in childcare for years I have watched mums torture themselves with guilt while trying to hold down a full-time job and juggle being a mummy. It's not pleasant sometimes especially when children are at the end of their best before date at the end of a long day/ week and are doing their exorcist impression (pea & ham soup spouting) and trying their hardest to show mummy up as incapable. In my eyes these mummies are doing an awesome job and need to remember that children don't hold grudges for real and grow up to appreciate what their Mums did for them. Thank you Mummy JoJo".

"Oh my days. I went to Maspie Den this weekend. Thank you so much. I thought I may have built it up in my head too much but it really was a magical, perfect day that

did not disappoint. Thank you. Thanks also for reminding me that busy people can be mindful too. We put far too much pressure on ourselves, don't we?"

TOOLKIT

Accept that it is OK to be busy and it is OK to love being busy. Maybe you love being busy with your job or volunteering. Perhaps you love being busy with DIY, cleaning, knitting, reading, keeping active. But always remember, as strong as you think you may be – you are not invincible.

Find a support network that helps you. This year, I have teamed up with Suzanne from The Batch Lady to get into mindful cooking. To be frank, the kitchen has been absolute chaos because I am a busy, working Mum like so many of us are. She gets how hectic life can be and she shares some fantastic time saving, nourishing recipes. We have collaborated and put a lot of video content and tips out together across social media. She was recently down filming with This Morning Live and I am so proud of her. Check out her website at www.thebatchlady.com.

Reach out to people and know that you are not alone. We are just trying our best.

I have not long finished recording a podcast with the amazing Konica from Diary of a Yoga Mummy. Konica thrives off being busy. But not so long ago her life changed in more ways than she thought possible.

What's your wellness worth?

"Picture this. You're working for a well-known
professional services firm. You've got a fab career,
one that you've worked hard for. You've been at this
firm for nearly fourteen years. You are trusted, have
expertise in your field, people contact you for advice and
guidance, you have a great boss who is understanding
and a brilliant team that you work with. You are by no
means perfect, still have lots to learn, there is a career
ladder that you can climb and you are encouraged to do
so, you have the support of those that work with you.
OK you have to travel, work in a fast-paced environment,
are pretty much always thinking about work and very
regularly check your work phone but that's just the way
it is, isn't it? You have the flexibility in your job that some
people would give their right arm for.
On the face of it a pretty good job right. Yes, absolutely.
So why did I so desperately want to get off?
Well see that's the thing. I didn't realise that I wanted
off until well it was almost too late. If I'm honest I should
have seen the signs. Looking back, I think they made
an appearance two years before I actually realised.
Yes two years. Instead I trundled on. I felt my patience
at home wearing thinner and thinner whilst at work
I was absolutely fine or so I thought. I loved my job, I
thrived in a fast-paced environment, it suited me and my
personality.

Until one day I woke up and thought I cannot do this anymore. The straw that broke the camel's back. Well mine was a haystack. I found out I was pregnant. The rug was pulled from underneath me. I was very busy at work, I had lots going on, how could I be pregnant as well. I could not do this anymore. I could not go on this way anymore. I phoned my boss. I can remember the conversation as if it was yesterday. He was dropping his kids off at school so I was on speaker phone. I asked him to call me back once he'd dropped them off. He must have heard something in my voice as he called me pretty much straight back. I was going to tell him that I wasn't feeling well (I wasn't!) and that I was going to take a few days off work but would check my e-mails and make sure everything was covered. Instead I broke down in tears told him I was seven weeks pregnant and that I just couldn't do this anymore. Clearly the hormones were in full force as I'm not entirely sure how coherent I was but I do remember him saying to me that it absolutely fine to take some time off and that he knew I was OK but why didn't I pop to the GP just in case. And I did. Turns out my mental wellness wasn't so well. Along with hyperemesis which kicked in around seven weeks and two days. I was 'stressed'.

Me? I am a strong person. I am a person that can get through anything. I've coped with stress, I've coped with high pressure situations before. Never ever did I think that I would be that person. Yet here I was. Hormones raging, chained to the sofa due to severe all-day sickness (!), the person signed off work and stressed. Mental wellness at zero. That's where it stayed until I had the energy physically and the willpower to start taking care of my mental wellness. Turns out that when all you can eat is one packet of beefy McCoy's a day due to feeling sick 24/7 your physical strength takes a while to build up! Thanks to my amazing hubby, who was pretty much a single parent for eleven weeks, and my family I managed to get through that period. Looking back, I should have seen the signs but when looking after yourself and your wellness, especially mental wellness, isn't a priority for you it's easy to ignore the signs. One thing I've learnt is to recognise my signs. For me that period was a bit of a voyage of self-discovery if you like. It's a bit of a grand way of saying that it gave me the chance to re-evaluate what I wanted and what was best for me and my family.

After much deliberation and discussion with my hubby I decided to leave the fabulous job that I'd worked so hard for, the job that I loved. I wanted to spend a little bit more time with my family. I wanted to be there for my family, be there for them as opposed to being half there and half thinking about the e-mail that I needed to send when they went to bed. I knew I still wanted to do something and I've found a new path setting up my own business teaching baby and toddler yoga. I'm passionate about being able to teach little ones how to relax and give their parents tools on how to relax their child. I knew how to relax, I love yoga, it really relaxes me. I just didn't do it when I should have. My mental wellness wasn't a priority for me. I don't want my kids to fall into the trap of not taking care of their mental wellness and not making it a priority.

I gave up my job, a good salary, I gave up my career. In the end I gave it up willingly. Why?

Because I realised that my

mental wellness is worth more than that.

I have a lump in my throat as I write this. The emotions are still pretty fresh even after all this time.

Thank you Konica for sharing and being so open and honest. I know that your words will help so many because this is real life.

You can follow her wonderful blog at

www.diaryofayogamummy.co.uk

CHAPTER 14

IT'S TIME FOR A MOJO INJECTION

Tonight
We are young
So let's set the world on fire
We can burn brighter
Than the sun
Fun

Right here, right now

Hello you,

Yes, you holding this book. Thanks for being here. You made it to the end, you stuck with me and for that I am delighted. Maybe it took you a while to get here, maybe you got here in one day. It doesn't matter. I'm just glad you are here now.

My passion is to encourage you to embrace who you are and not be afraid. We can't please everyone. Ice cream is great, but some people are lactose intolerant. Some people prefer sticky toffee pudding and extra toffee sauce (me). There is nothing worse than a dry sponge.

How is your balance these days? Perhaps you are tired, and you have had a tough day or week. Maybe you feel low and you don't know why. Maybe you do know. Are you allowing the negative thoughts in your sweet mind or voices from other people to drag you away from your mojo? That voice of guilt in your head called perfect Mum, perfect Auntie, husband, friend, son, daughter, wife. That guy you married who you thought was Prince Charming or that hot wife who seems like a totally different person now.

Maybe you are fed up with your job or you feel undervalued. Perhaps you have been caring for kids all day and you feel frazzled. Or maybe you are worrying about a sick family member or friend. Maybe you are missing someone desperately and the pain actually aches and comes back every so often, hitting you like a tidal wave. Perhaps someone told you that you are not good enough or tried to drag you away from being the champagne of the party. Did they call you larger than life? The thing is, it is impossible to be larger than life, life is abundant. Life can be so large when we embrace living it with our full mojo mindset.

Maybe you are fed up of people that see life as a competition. I have been there and it is exhausting. There is no competition. We are all unique. We are all capable. Some of the most inspirational people I have met came from absolutely nothing. There was no silver spoon, no love, no nurturing. There of course was a journey of healing but they clung onto their vision to make a change.

Perhaps you are desperate for a large glass of wine and a huge bit of cake, but you feel guilty about it or scared that you will lose control. Maybe you have just been looking through social media and you are comparing yourself to others. Their marriage, their friends, job, house, lifestyle, clothes, what they cooked for dinner. Maybe you are being judgmental of others and you can't help being full of anger or negative thoughts, instead of focusing on getting your mojo back.

Sometimes people look like they have the world at their feet. That doesn't mean that they don't struggle or doubt themselves. They hear all the critical thoughts too. Mental wellness does not discriminate. Often people with a life that looks perfect on paper are the ones that suffer. Nobody is immune, we all have a mind we need to nurture. We all need a daily mojo injection. Self-care is so underrated, and we need to practise it daily, with the same priority we give to brushing our teeth.

It is normal to have so much outwardly, but feet so empty and lost on the inside. It is normal for the mind to keep people up most of the night, mulling over things that don't really matter in the end. Things like money, trying to be enough for family and friends and what others think of us. We all have our own issues and voices going on in our minds.

Which negative voices are holding you back? Take a moment to be honest and reflect on those voices. Write them down if it helps. Then read this.

Those harsh voices do not belong in such a beautiful mind. A mind that is capable of helping you live a life you love. A mind that can allow you to have a happy mojo glow. A unique mind that is capable of making a huge difference. There is only one of you. You have the ability to be purely, authentically magical. The very best version of yourself.

The version where your eyes are sparkling. We are all born equal. We all have mojo magic in us.

Read this a few times until it sinks in. Highlight it. Believe it. Because it is true.

Remember that thoughts come and go but we do not have to act on them. Sometimes life throws us big fat, juicy lemons. Perhaps enough to make a crate of limoncello. Life can get really tough. Mental pain can physically hurt. We need tools to get us through the storm. We need armour. We all need our own toolkit.

Let's start by telling those thoughts to pipe down. Let them in and then show them the front door.

Right now, Bonnie and Charlie's eyes sparkle. They are living a happy life in their full mojo. They are amazing at being themselves.

Embracing their wonderfulness is a beautiful form of self-care. Because only when we really stop, only when we are as mindful and present as they are do we really get it. That's when our eyes are really open to a beautiful and magical world. You see, young children aren't afraid of looking foolish. They embrace people and adventure with open arms. It is a wonderful time, but as they grow those voices of self-doubt start creeping in. They start to compare. They start to lose a little of the magic.

I want my kids to keep the magic for as long as possible. I choose to join them. I choose to sing with the same passion that shines out of them in my voice and I choose to dance with their infectious energy and enthusiasm. I do it as often as I can and I share it on Instagram stories for all to see. Because it feels wonderful spreading a little bit of that mojo. I love being me. Maybe music doesn't float your boat as much. Maybe you prefer to get lost in art, knitting or scrabble. That's cool. Do it.

My kids inspire me to be excited when I write down words and create something wonderful. They inspire me to love as hard as they do and hug as tight. They inspire me to be as simple and honest and caring and fun. They inspire me to be as excited about an adventure.

Let me ask – who are you? Do you apologise for being you? Perhaps you tone it down or overcompensate? Why should you? Why should you not enjoy living your life as you? How wonderful. How beautiful to not be intimidated by others.

When we live our lives in ways that aren't congruent with our values, passions and abilities then we are dodging our best mojo. That sucks. I recognised when I was doing it. My gut feeling was crying out that something wasn't right. Be it a job, a relationship or an activity I didn't love. I stopped doing it.

I didn't want to follow other people's rules and styles. I didn't want to cover up my tattoos. I didn't want to put on an act. I didn't want to blend in with a black suit from Hobbs. I wanted to write and film. I wanted to inspire others and create content that had my stamp all over it.

What do you want to do?

I didn't want to be in a relationship where I wasn't accepted for being me. I need people who build me up and encourage me to be my own kind of champagne vintage. I am loving and passionate, at times messy, impatient, determined and timekeeping mad. I am wild, I am calm, I am unstoppable, I am gushy, I am tactile, I am open minded. I am spiritual, I am anxious, I am happy. I know who I am, and I know I am not perfect. I also know that nobody else is either. We don't need to be. Living in our mojo means accepting our strengths and weaknesses. It is about being real which in turn helps us to connect with others on a deeper level. This life is not a performance unless you are on the stage.

When we are being true, we are more resilient and we make better choices. We are more likely to put our money where our mouth is and stick to those goals. Being a goal digger = one huge mojo injection.

Hopes and dreams that are supressed by the opinions of others are gifts that are wasted. They destroy our worthiness and confidence. Living our lives in our mojo takes effort. It can feel uncomfortable. Get comfortable feeling uncomfortable. Sometimes it is hard to accept compliments. Sometimes it is scary to give them, even when we really want to.

Start giving more compliments and start accepting them too. Thank people and believe them. Accept people as they come. The more we fight against life and judge others, the harder we make it.

Remember that nothing we get brings permanent wellbeing. A marathon medal, a Porsche, a new, exciting relationship with a person (not prince). A new baby who before you know it will be starting school. A baby that no longer needs you at their beck and call. In the same way, stress won't last forever. No one experience we have on this earth is the be all and end all to life. Even if it feels that way right now.

It is possible to do amazing things when we feel sad or angry. Negative feelings are a normal part of life. I spoke recently at a talk about my heart pumping out of my chest before I went on live national TV. That anxiety didn't hold me back from grabbing the mic and speaking in front of millions of people. I still got the job done. It was OK. Until the live connection went down, but hey – not within my control.

It can be hard to truly accept things, and not over-analyse or keep asking why or thinking of things you could have done differently. Give yourself a bit of a break.

Your experiences are yours and yours alone. You will have your own unique, private life lessons. Be grateful to have had them and use them to help others. Those are the people I meet that are living in full, 100% mojo. They have scars, but they are using them to do incredible things. Embrace your scars. That will boost your wellbeing. It feels incredible to make a difference.

Follow your passions. What do you love to do? Schedule in time to do these things as often as you can. Do things that fuel your soul and you will have so much more to give.

Find a balance that works for you. Follow your gut. If you feel like something is starting to control you then take a break. Go on a detox, cut out sugar or booze for a bit. Replace coffee with green tea if you are starting to feel anxious. Put your phone away.

When your mind starts to feel anxious, it is your body telling you that something needs to change. Don't be afraid to challenge yourself. Don't pigeonhole yourself either. We can change, we can grow. Maybe you need more sleep, more self-love, less caffeine, less nights out drinking wine. Life is all about balance. Don't deprive yourself either.

If you are in a job that makes you sad, you do not have to stay there. Get focused, make a plan and chip away at it. Do something you love. Don't listen to the crowds. Be determined and you will get results. If you want it enough.

If you are happy in your job, embrace it. Be grateful for it every single day. So many people do not feel that way.

Tell the special people in your life that you love them. Force yourself to be present at points throughout the day. Embrace gushy mindfulness. Sit calmly and focus on the feel of their skin. The details on their face. The way they laugh, the way they talk.

Feel. Take yourself back to the moment you met. Why you were drawn to that person. Take yourself back to the day you held your child in your arms for the first time. That intense, overwhelming feeling of love and contentment. Hug more. A good hug is overrated.

Don't be intimidated by parents who find time to make scones. It's not that hard. Don't be intimidated by those who push you away because they are in mental or emotional pain. Don't be intimidated by people who look fitter. Don't be intimidated by your scars or other people's. Take people at face value. Don't be intimidated by tears. Cry to a beautiful piece of music. Embrace feelings. Feelings are beautiful.

Don't make up stories in your head when people fail to reply to your email. It's often not about you. We are all on our own journey and sometimes people are just very busy or poor at communicating. Don't take it personally.

Don't be intimidated by other people's talents, progress and strength. Encourage people who are achieving their goals. They may need it more than you know. Jealousy can be an evil, horrible thing. Tell any thoughts of jealousy to back off. Learn to be happy for people. Be inspired, not intimidated.

Imagine every day you woke up excited ready to go out and live? With sparkling eyes, ready to embrace a new day. A day that most people don't get to live. We made it, we are here. The chances of you being born are 1 in 400 trillion. You are already amazing.

My wish is that you choose to live. You choose to swim. You choose to tell the negative thoughts in that sweet head of yours to SHUT IT. Because, my friend, it's time you found your full mojo.

JoJo x

#mojoinjection

ACKNOWLEDGEMENTS

And you can tell everybody this is your song
It may be quite simple, but now that it's done
I hope you don't mind
I hope you don't mind that I put down in words
How wonderful life is, now you're in the world

Elton John

This is the hardest section as I could literally be here all day. I will thank as many of you as I can face to face or via private message over the next few months, but you already know I am beyond grateful for all the support and encouragement.

Thank you to Sean Patrick (that guy), my publisher for seeing the potential in me and the work that I do. You are an inspiration.

Thanks to Hubs with your epic blue eyes, my rock and the mojo glow I needed when I was starting to lose faith. Thanks for allowing me to be so honest when I write and create content. Thanks for being a beautiful soul; the kids and I are beyond lucky.

Thanks to my little butterfly Bonnie, for your smile and caring nature and for teaching me a whole new kind of unconditional love. You are a beautiful, caring and fun little person who lights me up.

Thanks to Charlie for that Cheeky smile that melts my heart every single day. You make me want to be a better person. I love watching you play, you are so full of life and right now watching you sleep is one of my favourite hobbies.

Thanks to my Dad aka Pop for teaching me compassion and encouraging me to always keep it real. You are one of a kind and a great laugh. I love dancing with you. I love how much you are enjoying my podcast. I'm so thankful to have you back, smiling and laughing and being you. This one's for Arthur!

Thanks to my Mum, the beautiful Violet, for teaching me strength, perseverance and true love, for being with Dad every step of the way for over fifty years. Your homemade soup, casseroles and pancakes always make me feel at home. Super Gran! Sorry you are not big on tattoos but the Violet flower on my back above the Arthur book is for you because you are an incredible person. Music notes shall be added to it soon. Thanks for singing me into the world that night in hospital. You are so strong Mum x

Thanks to 'superman' my Father in Law, Dave, for being such a fantastic role model and a great laugh. For giving me so much time to work on my passions and being so hands on. Cooking, cleaning, loving those magical and mental grandchildren. You will never know how loved you are.

To my Mother in Law for laughing through life's challenges and being so loyal and always honest. For washing our clothes and spinning them and loving our family so much. I love watching you dance and sing.

Thanks to my brother David for encouraging me to be the champagne of the party, writing such beautiful poetry. Oh, and you make a great curry and beef rendang. Physical distance will never be a barrier to our emotional closeness.

Thanks to my brother Iain aka Nini for making me laugh and sharing your wisdom and musical talent with me. You are one of a kind. You make a great rib of beef and do a mean waltz.

To the beautiful Glenda and Katie, for always encouraging me and putting up with my camera filming.

Thanks to all my **amazing** friends. I am so blessed. Thanks for all the advice and support. So many of you have inspired this book and I'm thankful for all the laughter and epic memories with you. Sorry I have been a bit off the radar as I focused on this huge life goal. Thanks for not taking it personally and still loving me, even when I take ages to reply to the group WhatsApp chats.

To my souly JJ for inspiring the mojo chat and my bibs Clara B for encouraging me to set up those social media accounts in the first place. To Flic and AJ for the support and banter.

To Nat for all the friendship, support, design work and opportunities you have put my way. I will always be your cheerleader. Creative, friendly and passionate indeed (www. alleramarketing.com). You are a true talent, and thanks for introducing me to Hubs and designing such lovely book launch invites.

Thanks to my monkey Cheeko for making me laugh – I think my love of comedy plays started with you when we were tiny. I love the Mummy JoJo/Edinburgh Castle picture you designed. You are a talented, hardworking artist.

www.cherithharrison.com

Thanks to the beautiful Rachael Lynch at Beautiful Bairns Photography for all the support. You are a wonderful person and such a talented photographer. Thanks for helping me create an honest and natural front cover shot that I totally love.

To the blogging and social media community and all the amazing people I have met recently. Thank you so much for your support. It's been amazing getting to know so many wonderful people and already having some of you on the podcast. This is just the start of an amazing adventure. What a tribe to be part of.

To my school gals. Thanks to Alana for coming to watch my runs, for being my cheerleader. For being there when I really needed you and having my back. To Sarah for your banter, it's like we are fifteen again when you come home from France. To Kat and Les, so proud of you medical girls and your top chat. Thanks for all the encouragement and FUN. Thanks for putting up with my selfies hahah x

To the lovely Emma R W for offering amazing advice when I first started writing this book. I love singing with you (and dinner parties).

To Iona for taking me to my favourite beach with those talents and chatting to my unconscious mind. What a journey we have been on so far, thanks for encouraging me to rock my mojo mindset. You are a true inspiration and it has been an honour to have you play such a special part of this book and podcast series one.

To everyone who contributed to this book and shared so much to help raise awareness, thank you for being so brave and so honest. I am eternally grateful.

Thanks to Angela from the Wellbeing Festival. I loved hosting what was an incredibly powerful event this year. You have been an amazing support and I really appreciate it. www.edinburghwellbeingfestival.com

Thanks to the very creative Mat Norbury for all the amazing filming fun and projects. Here's to many more and our mojo events. I love being on tour with you and such a talented production crew. You always keep me topped up with great coffee and you have great taste, water and wellness all the way!

Thanks to all the wonderful brands who have stuck behind me and supported me. A special shout out to the wonderful Wagamama for believing in me and sponsoring my podcast launch. The first place I finally used chopsticks. Mindful eating all the way! Looking forward to many more events with you.

Thanks to the amazing Borthwick castle for sponsoring my book launch. What a castle, what a team!

To David Lloyd for all the support. That outdoor pool will always be my happy place – water and wellness is a thing! I wrote a lot of my favourite content in the clubroom, fuelled by many a cracking cappuccino. Blaze classes are a game changer #blazetribe.

To Emma D, I have loved our deep conversations. Transformational dialogue is powerful, and you have challenged me in so many ways and given me new-found confidence and belief in myself. You are a wise, intelligent, intuitive Goddess and a fab business coach too. It is all about clarity baby.

Thanks to Michael Ulloa for having my back – I love your vision and believe you are doing really special things that will make a huge difference to the fitness industry. Thanks for encouraging me to stay strong, introducing me to beef jerky and of course all the fun vlogging. I love your authentic voice and you are a great singer too. You are always welcome on the podcast.

Thanks to Kaye Taylor, Steph Wilson and Jacqueline Hollows from Human Being TV. for inviting me to your three day "mind spa" all about the work of Sydney Banks. It was a game changer. Our thoughts are powerful but they do not have to define us.

Thanks to Emma O for being so honest and open about anxiety. Keep up all the fantastic work and awareness. It's been great getting to know you.

Thanks to Gavin Oattes for the public speaking tips and general epic motivational content. Please come on the podcast soon and we can sing 'Crazy Crazy Nights'.

Thanks to Suzanne aka The Batch Lady for helping me get my freezer sorted. Perfect Mum is delighted. I love cooking with you and filming of course.

Thanks to the very lovely Jo Lee from Valour coaching. You are a wonderful person. Thanks for sharing your wise words and advice about social media, especially for teenagers. I shall cherish my mojo candle.

Thank you to anyone who has ever liked, commented, read or watched any of my content. You are the reason I do what I do. S.W.A.L.K. JoJo x

Please feel free to contact JoJo anytime –

mummyJoJoblog@gmail.com

Facebook - @mummyJoJouncut

Instagram - @mummyJoJouncut

Twitter - @mummyJoJouncut

Thank you so much for reading my book. Please connect with me across social media and feel free to hashtag the hell out of #mojoinjection or #mummyjojouncut.

Lightning Source UK Ltd.
Milton Keynes UK
UKHW02f2254230818
327721UK00011B/820/P